An Inspiring Story About an
African Tradition
of Teamwork and Collaboration

Stephen C. Lundin
and Bob Nelson

BROADWAY BOOKS
NEW YORK

BROADWAY

Copyright © 2010 by Dr. Bob Nelson and Stephen Lundin

Published in the United States by Broadway Books,
an imprint of the Crown Publishing Group,
a division of Random House, Inc., New York.
www.crownpublishing.com

BROADWAY BOOKS and the Broadway Books colophon are trademarks
of Random House, Inc.

Library of Congress Cataloging-in-Publication Data
Lundin, Stephen C., 1941–
Ubuntu! : an inspiring story about an African tradition
of teamwork and cooperation / Stephen C. Lundin and
Bob Nelson. — 1st ed.
p. cm.
1. Employee motivation. 2. Teams in the workplace.
3. Interpersonal relations. 4. Corporate culture.
5. Management. I. Nelson, Bob, 1956– II. Title.
HF5549.5.M63L864   2010
658.4'022—dc22   2009042269

ISBN 978-0-307-58788-6

Printed in the United States of America

DESIGN BY BARBARA STURMAN

2 4 6 8 10 9 7 5 3 1

First Edition

To all the women and men who go to work each day and bring their humanity with them. They make a contribution to their organization by doing what they do, and they make a contribution to the world by being who they are while they do it.

We believe that in the long run the special contribution to the world by Africa will be in the field of human relationship. The great powers of the world may have done wonders in giving the world an industrial and military look, but the great gift still has to come from Africa—giving the world a more human face.

—**STEVE BIKO,** 1970

Political activist who died for his beliefs

PREFACE

No matter what part of the world we live in, we all share similar basic values and desires: We cherish family, love our children, want to make the most of our lives and make a difference in the world, seek a sense of security, and enjoy our friendships.

But despite the fact that we have similar values and essentially the same genes, the focus of our attention is often on our differences—Arab and Jew, Protestant and Catholic, Muslim and Christian, liberal and conservative—and the color of our skin—black, brown, red, yellow, or white.

The authors share a dream—a dream of a world where being human is such a big idea that differences seem small by comparison. We share a dream of a world where children grow up accomplishing worthy goals together, a world where "love thy neighbor" is less a euphemism and more a deeply held belief, and a world where simply being human is reason enough to be treated with respect.

We are also realists. We know that sharing a dream is not enough; action is required. And we look to an institution with which we are familiar to become a catalyst for this change. We look to business.

There are good reasons to do so. In our lifetime we have watched businesses outgrow the arbitrary borders separating one country from another and span the world. We see this global interconnectedness and wonder if it might be the needed platform. What better place to start than at work, a place where most of us spend the majority of our waking hours?

We have observed over the years that organizations loudly and proudly proclaim that "people are our most important asset," a statement that is often displayed prominently in a company's mission, literature, or annual report. But in reality, only a few organizations fully deliver on this promise. This gap has both human and financial consequences.

The evidence is clear that satisfied, more committed employees help improve a company's performance. In a recent study that analyzed the financial returns of *Fortune*'s 100 Best Companies to Work for in America, the organizations that made the cut had a 14 percent annual return over a six-year period, compared with a 6 percent return for the overall market. Another recent study showed that companies with higher employee satisfaction scores had a 700 percent higher shareholder return.

We have written this book because we think that the philosophy we describe can help organizations deliver on their commitment to people and in so doing become more successful in reaching their strategic goals. We believe an outcome of this effort will be a more human and connected world and the return of civility. Is it possible that a more civil world and success in business have common roots?

What if today's organizations could play a key role in doing what politics and religion alone have not been able to accomplish alone: bring us together in the pursuit of purposeful lives while treating each other with respect, compassion, and dignity. The story that follows describes how such a transformation could begin. Although it is fictional, it is based on real-life experiences of the authors and is consistent with the findings of our research.

—STEVE LUNDIN, *Vero Beach, Florida*
BOB NELSON, *San Diego, California*

PART ONE

A PROBLEM EMERGES
AT WORK

A Durban Morning

The sun is low on the horizon on a lush and brilliant South African morning. The hills in the distance shimmer with a hundred shades of green. On a dirt footpath paralleling a dusty rural road outside of Durban, two men approach each other from opposite directions. Their history could be the history of men and women meeting on dusty roads anywhere in the world. Each man brings a tribal heritage or past that includes at least one violent chapter. Today, as they near the point of intersection, each is aware of the past difficulties between their tribes, and there is an instant of anxiety. The moment passes quickly, replaced by something much larger.

As the men pause for a moment of greeting, the harsh history of the conflict between their clans and the more recent and equally harsh shared memories of apartheid become simply background for their wide smiles and heartfelt salutations.

"Sawa bona," says the first—"I see you."

"Sikhona," replies the second—"I am here." And with this simple exchange they bring each other into existence, for it is their belief that a person is a person only through human connection, through recognition of one another.

In this magic moment, one member of the human race has acknowledged another, and an ancient African philosophy comes to life, a philosophy that is stronger than past conflicts and more powerful than the pain of apartheid: the unifying spirit of Ubuntu.

Ubuntu—the ancient African philosophy that draws on the fact that we are one human family. We are brothers and sisters, traveling this earth together. When one man is poorly fed, all are malnourished. When one is abused, we all feel the pain. When a child suffers, the tears wash over us all. By recognizing the humanity of one another, we recognize our unbreakable bond—our unbreakable link to the whole of humanity.

BullsEye Financial Center,
Barrington, Illinois

WEST ON U.S. 90 from Chicago, just before the exit to Elgin, lies the once sleepy farming town of Barrington, where horses and other agricultural animals now share the land with office buildings. With Chicago's urban sprawl approaching the Wisconsin border, Barrington became the home of a variety of corporate campuses and assorted office complexes. The tallest of the new buildings is the BullsEye Financial Center, where the financial operations of BullsEye have been consolidated. BullsEye, a large global retailer employing over 200,000 men and women in hundreds of locations, sells virtually every item imaginable for the home and the home occupant. If you wear it, sit on it, wash dishes or clothing with it, watch it, or use it as a tool, you can find it at BullsEye. Or you can lease it, mortgage it, or insure it at a convenient BullsEye Financial Kiosk. Among the operations housed in the Financial Center are the leasing division, the mortgage group, and the employee financial products department.

On the twenty-second floor, Barb Robbins was stewing. Her staff had informed her that the applications received from the credit department were incomplete. *Again,* she thought.

John Peterson, manager of the credit department, had been one of her best employees when he worked for her. He was reliable and hardworking and rarely made a mistake. Because of his strong work ethic and the quality of his work she recommended him for a promotion when a new manager's position was created during the recent consolidation. Credit was John's specialty, and so it seemed like a natural for him to manage the credit group.

I did it to myself, Barb thought, eyeing the disappointing results from John's group. She couldn't fault her decision—John had been an outstanding employee and a good person as well. I remember how passionate he was when he talked about his family and the work he was doing with physically challenged children. His brother had cerebral palsy, so he knew firsthand about the challenge of such a debilitating disability. He gave tirelessly of himself. But for some reason, as a manager, he seems to have lost his way. He has lost some of that camaraderie as well. I can't let the substandard work in his department go—my customers are being affected. But before I take this to Nancy, I'm going to talk to him face to face. I owe him that much.

Barb's group was one of five internal finance groups served by John's credit team. Her department had scheduled closings with customers whose applications rested incomplete in the cart. She was facing the real possibility of disappointing those customers.

Barb had worked at BullsEye through all kinds of markets. But the recent financial meltdown was the most devastating she'd ever seen. Everyone at the company was under pressure these days to make his or her numbers, and her clients were especially jumpy with the recent erosion of their retirement savings and the value of their homes. Their confidence in *everything* financial was fragile at best. She did not want to add to their stress with delays.

She headed for the elevator and rode up two floors, pushing a file cart full of rejected applications before her. She knocked on the open door of John's office and was startled by his appearance. A meticulous dresser, John looked like he had slept in his clothing. His eyes were bloodshot.

"John, what's wrong?"

"Hi, Barb. I'm sorry—I know I look terrible. Come on in. How are you doing? I don't see you much anymore. Do you have plans for the long Memorial Day weekend?"

"We are staying at home this weekend. I would love to socialize, John, but I have something I need to discuss with you."

"I know why you are here, Barb. I'm just sick about the sloppy work my department has given you. Ralph has already been up here, and I expect to see Tanya and the other group leaders soon. Or perhaps they went straight to Nancy. I have asked the staff to stay around and help clean up the mistakes, but most just put their heads down and mumbled something about holiday plans."

Barb was concerned about John's appearance—he looked terrible—but felt that she had to steel herself for what was to follow.

"John, you know how much our group relies on the work your team does. BullsEye's commitment to its customers is a one-week turnaround. But we can't close these loan applications without complete files. Our deadline for this group of customers is Tuesday. And some of these files are for BullsEye employees, John!"

"I know, Barb. I'll take care of it. I blame myself for this. Usually I stay late for an hour or two at the end of the day to look over my staff's work. If I need to, I come in early to correct any mistakes. I've been distracted this week. But it won't happen again."

Barb softened. "Distracted?"

"My dad had a stroke last weekend. This week has been crazy. He's out of intensive care and probably will be moved to the rehab section of the hospital in a day or two. He will need to learn how to walk and talk again. I guess moving to rehab is good news—he is lucky to be alive."

"I'm so sorry, John. I know you've had your ups and downs with your father, but I also know you love him."

"Yeah. It's a bummer. He was planning to visit the World War II Memorial in Washington, D.C., this weekend with some of his war buddies. You know, the greatest generation and all that. Instead, he's stuck in Methodist Hospital. And since my mom can't drive, I'm the one on call to take her to the hospital."

"What's the prognosis?"

"Well, he's eighty-six. A stroke at that age takes its toll. Even if the rehabilitation is successful, I don't think he will ever drive again. On the other hand, he probably shouldn't have been driving anyway. The doctors say he should be able to walk with a walker and his speech should improve. He's a tough old bird. Anyway, I've been at the hospital a lot this week, so I haven't been able to catch up as much.

"Can your wife help? Alice?"

John looked down in embarrassment. "Oh—I thought everyone knew—the gossip mill and all. I moved out. My wife asked for a trial separation a month ago. I was pretty devastated, to be honest. And now, with my dad, it's been . . . hectic. May hasn't been a great month for me."

"I'm so sorry," Barb said, seeing how much pain John was in.

"Alice felt that I was never home enough—she didn't see the point anymore. Essentially, she told me she thought my job was more important to me than my family. I don't really know what to do, Barb. I know I put in too many hours, but I've barely been able to keep my head above water as it is with the new job. I don't know—the younger people on my staff just don't seem to have the same work ethic. On the other hand, I can see what all the hours I've put in are doing to my relationship with my wife and daughter."

Barb didn't know what to say. She felt sorry for John, but she also knew John's staff problems were his own creation. She made a motion to leave, thinking about her own work and the coming weekend.

"I'll stay this weekend and finish these files myself, Barb. My sister is flying in to help with Dad; I can spend the three-day weekend at the office if I need to. I'm three times as fast as my staff, as I keep telling them; I'll be able to make the corrections."

7

Suddenly John's phone rang. "Hello, John here. Yes, I expected a call from you. Everything is under control. No problem. I'm talking with Barb right now. I'm on top of it. Things will be ready by Tuesday when we open for business. You want to see me first thing Tuesday morning? Sure, I can do that. Okay. Great."

"That was Nancy," he said, referring to their mutual boss. "Are those the unacceptable files in the cart?"

"Some of the files, John. The rest are outside of my office. Do you mind getting them?"

"It's the least I can do. Again, I am so sorry. I just ran out of time with Dad and all."

8

Barb Talks Straight

OVER THE last year Barb had observed the evolution—or lack of evolution—of John's management style. Barb was also aware of how frustrated Nancy, their boss, was with the frequent quality problems in John's department. She wondered if John could be in jeopardy of losing his job, so she decided to talk straight with him. Given their past relationship, it was, she realized, the least she could do.

"John, the way you run your department—it doesn't have to be this way."

"What do you mean?"

"Look, the members of your team don't enjoy performing poorly and being looked down on by the other departments any more than you do. I have never met a human being that didn't want to do a good job and feel proud about the team with whom he or she worked."

"Barb, that's easy for you to say. You have an all-star cast. My people just seem to want a paycheck. And they don't seem to be willing to work for it."

"The members of my team aren't like that at all."

John was startled by Barb's directness. "You're right. I have noticed how hard your team works and how well they work together. My department has never had the same team approach that yours has. I'm not you. I can't be a den mother to my staff. They are adults—I expect them to do their job."

"What are you suggesting? Do you think my staff is productive because I treat them like children?"

9

ubuntu!

We tell ourselves stories to explain the events in our lives. Being connected to others provides a necessary opportunity to challenge stories that might be hurting our performance and inhibiting our growth.

"Well . . . ah . . . no, that's not it."

"Then what?"

"Look, your people seem to genuinely like you. I just don't have that kind of gung-ho personality or rapport with my group. I feel the people in my department have a job to do, and I expect them to do it without my holding their hand. I'm not running a popularity contest. I expect them to earn their paychecks by doing the work they are assigned and doing it well, just as I do."

"And how is that approach working for you?"

John looked down, embarrassed. "I admit I've been distracted. The fact is, if I don't ride herd on them or follow up on every detail, I feel the department will fall apart. Maybe I need to come down with a heavier hand and get rid of the nonperformers. Whip my department into shape again. Those who can't or won't do the work will be gone."

"But this isn't a new development, is it, John? Has what you're suggesting worked in the past? And how successful are you when you need to recruit a new team member?"

At that, the bluster went out of John's sails and he visibly slumped, looking even more tired. "Actually, I have two openings right now and there are no applicants. No one seems to want to work for me anymore. My last hire was an applicant from Africa."

As if on cue, a young man heading for the elevator called out, "Good night, John. Have a nice weekend. Have a nice weekend, Ms. Robbins."

"And you, too, ah . . ."

"Simon."

"Thank you, Simon. I will. Call me Barb."

"Sorry, Ms. Barb. Have a good weekend. We're supposed to have beautiful weather."

John mumbled something half to himself about spending his weekend cleaning up others' messes and didn't look up. When Simon overheard what he had said, a panicked look replaced his smile as he hurried for the elevator.

"That's the guy I was talking about. He's from a Zulu clan in Africa; he ran a business in Pretoria. He is working on his MBA at Illinois State."

"He seems quite nice."

"I don't expect too much from him with his class schedule and the cultural differences, but at least he's a warm body. My guess is after he gets his degree, he'll leave. And in the meantime, he'll be too tired from his classwork to do much of a job while he is here."

"Simon. Oh, yes, I remember Simon—his work was excellent! None of the rejected files are his. In fact, we went ahead and scheduled his clients first because no re-work was necessary."

"Well, I'm surprised. He hangs around a lot with Ricardo, the chief complainer in the department. It's just a matter of time before he picks up the same bad habits."

Barb had had just about all the negativity she could stand for one day. She said a quick good night. As she entered the elevator, John called out, "I'll be caught up after the long weekend, Barb, even if I have to pull an all-nighter."

As the door shut and the packed elevator headed down, Barb thought to herself, John seems clueless about how to work with his staff. He was so excited about becoming a manager. But now I'm not so sure he's well suited for the job. I'm glad Nancy has decided to step in. Hey, a three-day weekend—I'm out of here.

And with the thought of the family picnic before her, she smiled and put John out of her mind.

Schaumburg, Illinois

Twenty miles outside of Chicago, at a small table outside an upscale coffee shop near the Schaumburg Mall, two men briefly decided to escape the confines of their nearby office building to share a quick cup of coffee. It was a spectacular spring day in mid-May; shirtsleeves replaced winter jackets and suit coats.

The two colleagues worked in the operations department of BullsEye; the tall building towering above them was the headquarters of the retail enterprise.

"On days like today I seem to think of her more often, Rolando."

"Alexandra, my friend?"

Steve looked at his buddy and nodded. "She loved the sunny warm days of spring, with all their promise. I miss her. I miss her contagious enthusiasm for life." They sat in silence for a moment, honoring Alexandra's memory. Steve had lost his fiancée less than a year ago to a rare illness; the pain was still raw.

Almost in relief, they moved the conversation to the familiar territory of work and the foibles of their boss.

"Can you believe the latest?" Rolando said.

"What?"

"We are being asked to participate in a motivation program developed for the automobile industry, redesigned by some clever marketing type as a tool to promote productivity. It's set up as a kind of game."

"White-collar productivity is quite trendy in management schools these days. That is why I favor blue shirts," Steve said with a smile.

"You might try starch," Rolando needled him. "You can now buy it at BullsEye."

"You don't think I look professional enough? At least I'm not wearing sandals."

"These are loafers, not sandals. Do you want to know about the game or not?"

"Please. The suspense is killing me."

"Each of us will get our own game card. Every day there will be a clue in the company newsletter that corresponds to one of the cells on the game card. You watch for the clues and fill in the cells."

"I can see where an incentive program like that would help sell cars, but what we do is a long way from the showroom floor. What's behind this new initiative? Maybe they just want us to read the newsletter."

"I think BullsEye is looking for anything that will motivate our employees. I have heard a rumor that the employee survey results were pretty bad. The good thing is that there are prizes you can win when you play the game."

"I'm all ears."

"Well, the first two prizes are what you'd expect. Fill five cells on your game card and you get a company pen. Ten cells and you 'win' a wall poster with the program logo—complete with rules about where you can hang it in your cube."

"I guess they haven't forgotten how creative we got with the results and tactics poster we received—they didn't appreciate how many interesting ways there are to use the acronym RATS. I think the humor was lost on top management."

"But when the game card is full . . ." Rolando went on.

"Drumroll, please . . ."

"You get a fifty dollar gift certificate for BullsEye products and the opportunity to write a short essay on why our people matter, for the grand prize. The top two essays win the grand prize."

"Which is?"

"A weeklong, all-expenses-paid trip to South Africa, including an African safari and a tour of Johannesburg."

"Whoa. Not bad; I'd settle for that."

"The winning employees' bosses are invited as well."

"And what is second prize, two weeks with your boss in Toledo?"

They laughed in spite of themselves.

Rolando glanced at his watch. "Time to head back, my friend."

"Right. See you tomorrow, buddy. I'll bet you I get my card filled before you do."

"That won't be hard. I'm on vacation next week."

As they ambled back to the BullsEye building, they talked about Rolando's upcoming fishing trip in northern Ontario. But Rolando had piqued Steve's interest; Steve couldn't stop thinking about the new corporate initiative. Usually such programs were a source of cynicism within the company. But in this case, he had to admit he was intrigued, given the grand prize.

Simon Is Hurting

WHEN SIMON left the building, his stomach and his mind were in knots. *What did John mean? Was my work not so good?*

While he was waiting for the bus to take him to the train station, John's comment was all Simon could think about. *John has to work this weekend because our work was not good enough.*

Simon's wife, Sarah, greeted him as he walked up the short sidewalk to the common entrance of their triplex—1,100 square feet of the most luxurious apartment they had ever lived in. They had been renting an apartment in South Chicago when they got lucky—a professor at Illinois State had gone on sabbatical and decided to sublease his apartment. He wanted married students only, and Simon and Sarah were the first to apply. With no increase in their rent, they had improved their living conditions vastly. They kept the triplex neat as a pin, and they helped maintain the small yard. In fact, the yard looked so beautifully kept that the neighbors often stopped and complimented them, thinking they were the owners.

Sarah, who at six feet tall held herself with a proud carriage, had fled the turmoil of her homeland in the Congo and ended up in Pretoria, South Africa. It was there she had met Simon at a church gathering. Before

15

long, they had fallen deeply in love, and eventually they had married. They frequently gave thanks for their good fortune.

Every morning at 4 A.M. Sarah took a bus to the commuter train to get to the airport, where she worked in a parking lot booth collecting fees. She had scheduled her classes at Oak Brook Community College in the late afternoon.

As Simon greeted her this evening, he said, "Sarah, my love. I come home with a heavy heart today." And he described John's last words as he left work.

"Simon, I am so sorry. There must be some mistake. I know you do good work."

By the time they finished dinner, Simon had decided to miss his final exam in organizational psychology that was scheduled on Saturday and go back to the office. The professor who taught the class, Dr. Ling, was a good person, he told Sarah, and they hoped she would allow him to reschedule the exam. Simon really saw no choice. It was what he felt he had to do. It was Ubuntu, the ancient life philosophy, that guided him.

Memorial Day Weekend,
BullsEye Barrington

JOHN ARRIVED at the Bullseye Financial Center in a sleep-deprived daze as he registered at the security desk. Here I am again on a Saturday. What is wrong with this picture? Why can't I get my employees to do their work?

"There is someone else up there, sir."

"Sorry, what did you say?"

"There is already a gentleman up on the twenty-fourth floor."

"Oh. Curious." John looked down at the sign-in sheet and saw Simon's name. "What the heck is he doing here?"

"He didn't say, sir. Is everything all right? Should I call security?"

"You are security," John said.

"That makes it an easy call—I almost always get through." The guard smiled.

"Enough!" John said, grinning for the first time that day. "Everything is fine; I'm just surprised, that's all. I see you are still wasting your time at those comedy clubs. Thanks for the smile, Turk."

"Always a pleasure, sir. Are you still teaching swimming to the kids down at the Courage Center? I have a child with spina bifida who goes there."

"I remember. Sadly, I haven't had time since I became a manager."

"Sorry to hear that, but I can understand."

As John rode up the elevator to the twenty-fourth floor he thought, Why do I have such a good relationship with the security guard and the cleaning crew but such a poor relationship with my own staff?

Simon sat at his desk working on some folders while he waited for John to arrive. He looked up as he heard John approach his cube.

"Simon. What brings you to the office? I thought you had a Saturday class."

Simon seemed surprised that John knew about his

class. Looking at him, John said, "Who do you think signs off on your tuition reimbursement?"

Simon smiled. "Thanks, Boss. The final exam is today, but I hope the professor will let me reschedule it."

"And why would you want to do that? Forget to study?"

Simon looked confused for a moment and then said with pride, "Oh, no. I study very hard and get good grades."

"So why are you here?"

"I am here to help."

John looked startled, and all he could say was, "Oh."

"I heard you say our work was not good. It isn't fair that you would have to work on the weekend because of my poor work."

It was John's turn to look confused.

"When you were talking to Ms. Barb, I heard you say you had to clean up the mess left by us this weekend. I would like to help."

What has my loose tongue done this time? John thought.

"It's okay, Boss?"

"Simon, I'm embarrassed. Your work was fine. After you left, Barb said no rework was necessary on any of your files. Unfortunately, half of the other applications need to be reworked. I was just ranting about how most of the work was unacceptable, but your work was fine. Go to class, Simon. I am sorry for the misunderstanding."

"I wondered why I couldn't find my files. I am pleased my work was acceptable. But I will stay and help."

"Why?"

"It doesn't make any difference if it was my work or someone else's work. We are all in this together as a department. I want to help. It is *Ubuntu*."

"What?"

"Ubuntu."

John smiled in confusion. "Ubuntu or no Ubuntu, I am glad to have your help. Please, call me John. Let's get to work, and maybe I won't have to come in tomorrow."

"You mean maybe *we* won't have to come in tomorrow."

"Ubuntu?"

Simon smiled. "Ubuntu."

ubuntu!

Ubuntu means we're all in this together.

Simon and John Finish the Rework

B Y TWO O'CLOCK the last file was complete. At least half of the rework had to do with credit adjustments. It was not a complicated process, just an exacting one. John was surprised to find that Simon worked as fast as he did.

"Thank you, Simon. You are a good worker."

Simon lowered his head self-consciously.

"What's wrong?"

"You said 'thank you.'"

"Of course. Instead of two days working alone, we finished the rework in less than a day and have the rest of the weekend for ourselves. Thank you."

"I have not heard this before."

John was startled by Simon's disclosure. "Do you mean others haven't thanked you for your work before? I have never said 'thank you'?"

"It's all right, John, I don't mind. I know you are busy."

"Well, I mind, Simon. Being busy is no excuse—I don't say thank you often enough. I guess I haven't been in the habit of thanking my staff for doing what they are paid to do. But this was above and beyond the call of duty, Simon. Let me take you to a late lunch."

"That's okay; I have a snack in here." Simon held up his Illinois State backpack.

"Save that for another time, Simon. I am going to treat you to lunch at the Sky Room in the mall."

"I have heard of the Sky Room, but I have never been there. And I *am* as hungry as a dog."

John smiled for the second time that day. "I think you mean hungry as a wolf."

"Yes, hungry as a wolf. I love the way Americans talk."

ubuntu!

Being busy is no excuse for avoiding the things that matter most.

Simon Talks about Africa

M OST OF the lunch crowd had left by the time Simon and John arrived at the Sky Room. They took a table by the window and looked at the menu. After ordering, John looked over at Simon and said, "You're a good employee, Simon. I bet they didn't teach you that in the MBA program at Illinois State."

"I have learned many things in the MBA program, but not how to work hard. I was raised on a small farm in rural South Africa. Hard work was required from each of us kids in order for our family to survive. We did not own the land, and so there was a limit on how much money we could generate farming.

"When I was old enough I decided to help the family by starting a small business in Pretoria. I had three older brothers and three sisters to help with the farm. After a year my business was doing well enough that I was able to provide financial assistance to my family and begin taking classes at the university. In my small business, working hard meant that I had enough money to help my family, had enough to eat, and had the tuition for school."

"What was your business?"

"I had a sewing factory; we manufactured African garments for sale and for export."

"You said 'we.' Did you have partners?"

"Yes—everyone who worked at the factory."

Noticing John's confused look, Simon added, "In the U.S. a small business owner would say 'I' to demonstrate ownership. In my tradition we use the word 'we,'

21

because even though I owned the business, at work we were a family, and as such, everyone was important."

"I see."

"There was retail space in the front of the factory for the occasional tourists. It sounds like a big deal, but the total square footage of the entire factory was less than 700 square feet. There were no walls, so you could stand in the retail space and see the whole factory. Tourists were attracted to seeing how we made the garments, to that sort of authentic African business experience, and our retail business grew."

"What happened to it?"

"I gave my brother Nigel a half interest in the business so I could come to America. He now runs the factory and store."

"Was it hard to leave behind something you had successfully built?"

"I was given an opportunity to attend Illinois State University. It had always been my dream to come to America."

"But in Pretoria you ran your own business. Here you work for a modest salary with a boss who doesn't even say thank you."

"The amount I am paid for one day's work here is more than I made in a week from the business in Pretoria. And it was a successful business. America is an amazing place. I don't think those who live here realize how amazing."

"I'm afraid we take a lot for granted in America, Simon."

"I am happy to be here. And I thank you for lunch."

"I think you'll love the wild rice soup and walleye you ordered. Walleye is the state fish in my home state of Minnesota. Just watch out for the small bones."

A Conversation at the Mall

JOHN AND Simon had finished eating and were sitting comfortably at the table, sipping their coffee. John realized he liked this young man Simon. While they were working so hard together that morning, a bond had formed between them. John hadn't experienced that kind of camaraderie since college, and he realized how much he enjoyed it. That sense of connection and teamwork was not something he often experienced at BullsEye.

23

ubuntu!

To engage another person in an authentic way releases the most powerful energy on the planet.

"Simon, tell me more about yourself. What do you do for fun?"

"My schoolwork takes most of my free time. My wife, Sarah, and I go to the movies occasionally to celebrate getting good grades in our course work. There is a theater near campus that shows old movies for a dollar. The movies are new to us, so it is a good value. Recently, I entered the contest at BullsEye. That was fun."

"What contest is that?"

"It is called OPM—Our People Matter. There are prizes for the winners. Do you not know about it? I filled out a game card and wrote a short essay."

"The acronyms in our company drive me crazy. I must have missed it. I've been too busy to pay attention to headquarters' new initiatives. Simon, let me ask you something. When you ran your business, did you ever have workers who weren't motivated to work hard?"

"Yes. That is a problem in Africa and everywhere, I think. In South Africa, blacks, coloreds, and Indian peoples were oppressed for so long that when apartheid ended with the election of Nelson Mandela and we received our freedom, many were not ready for the change. Work was associated with oppression. Many thought that having freedom meant they no longer had to work. They expected the government to take care of them. They just didn't understand about economics and the responsibilities that come with freedom. Their feelings were understandable but a problem for me because I had a business to run."

"I only know about apartheid thirdhand. At the time, Africa seemed a long way away from my life."

"Mandela was elected president on April 27, 1994. He was seventy-six, and Bishop Tutu was sixty-two. That day was the first time in their lives either had voted. Before then, under apartheid, blacks, coloreds, and Indians in South Africa could not vote, and they were not allowed to live in white neighborhoods."

"That does put it in perspective. We often don't think about our freedoms in the U.S."

"You asked about worker motivation. It was a problem in our business. I had some success over time, but I wish I knew then what I know now."

"How so?"

"The MBA program I am in has taught me much about managing and motivating people. I now have management concepts that help me understand my experiences."

John said, "I come from the school of hard knocks, as you probably have guessed. After I graduated college at the University of Wisconsin, I joined BullsEye in the finance department and worked my way up. I don't have an MBA." John looked reflective for a moment. "But if I were to be honest with myself, the school of hard knocks hasn't been serving me too well lately. You know what the situation is at the office. Our department is constantly behind in its work, and too much of our work is not at the level it needs to be. Frankly, I think I'm in trouble. As a manager, it's my job to make sure the department runs efficiently and smoothly. Is there anything that you learned in your MBA courses that might help me?" asked John.

"I am just a student, Boss. You are the manager—it is something I hope to be someday."

"But you already have been a manager—an owner—in Pretoria."

"Yes. But I wasn't conscious of being a manager at the time. I was simply trying to run the business. I didn't even know there was a thing called management. I now realize there is much more to being a good manager; it is something I want to achieve some day."

"Well, Simon, I may not be a manager much longer if things continue to go the way they went this week. Is there anything that you think might help me with my employees? I can't seem to motivate them to work hard."

Simon looked a bit nervous and unsure about how to respond.

"I'm serious, Simon."

"There is one thing I learned in Africa that may be helpful. And there are many things I have learned in the MBA program. Where do you want me to start?"

"Start with Africa. I am familiar with some of what they teach in business schools."

"Are you sure you don't want me to go over my notes on motivation theory?"

"Positive. I have learned many of the things you are studying at the management classes we offer at BullsEye University. What I know nothing about is what you brought with you from Africa."

Ubuntu

IN A word, what I brought with me from Africa is Ubuntu. Ubuntu is a part of me—it is a part of us all. It is about teamwork and brotherhood. It is finding that part of you that connects with other people and bringing it to life."

"All I know is that you came to work today to help me. And you said you were doing it because of Ubuntu."

"Yes. Here is what Ubuntu means to me. If you have work to do on the weekend in order for our team to succeed, then I have work to do, too. When you struggle, the Ubuntu in me reaches out to give you a hand. If you wander into my village with nothing to eat, our villagers will provide you with food. Why? Because at the deepest level we are all brothers and sisters. We are all a part of the human family. If one of us hurts, we all hurt.

"Ubuntu is a philosophy that considers the success of the group above that of the individual. It says that we exist because of our connection to the human community. I am a person through other human beings.

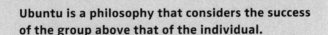

Ubuntu is a philosophy that considers the success of the group above that of the individual.

"Ubuntu is like the air I breathe. I don't have to think about it because it is always present. I would have trouble describing the air around me. But if the air was removed, I would notice immediately.

"So the community is more important than one's self?" John asked. "Don't we all have to succeed first individually?"

"Not necessarily. Let me give you an example. When the greed of a few individuals brought the financial systems of the world to their knees, did you support those individuals to do as they wished? Or did you fear for the community, for society, as a whole?"

"I was angry and afraid. My retirement account fell to half of what it was before the collapse because of the self-serving actions of a few. And a lot of people lost their jobs. I see what you are saying. Had we balanced the well-being of the community with the rights and actions of individuals, the financial community might have avoided this crisis. But how does Ubuntu work at a personal level?"

"While Ubuntu is a part of the fabric of Africa, it comes alive one individual at a time. It lives inside each of us who promotes the well-being of others and believes in the equality of all and our connection to the entire human race."

"So I have to find Ubuntu inside of me?"

"Yes. That is where you will find it."

ubuntu!

**The first step in bringing Ubuntu to life is discovering it in your own heart.
Ubuntu comes from our natural energy within.**

"Let me give you an example. America loves its sports teams—as do people all over the world. Some teams are dominated by one or two talented players. But the teams that win the championships usually have to find a way to get beyond their focus on a few individual stars and become a genuine team, working together. Some team members may have more talent and make bigger salaries, but on the court or on the field those differences take a backseat to the interests of the team. And that motivates all the members. They are all respected; they all have an important role to play in winning.

"I read that the coach of the Boston Celtics identified Ubuntu and its principles as one reason they were able to win a world championship.

"One of the things I believe I did well when I ran my business came naturally because it was a deeply held belief. I recognized all who worked with me as equal fellow human beings, and for that reason I gave them unconditional respect. I was no better than they; I was just the boss. So even though I had yet to learn about management, the gift of Ubuntu that I had learned as a young man allowed me to succeed as a manager.

"What the MBA program has helped me understand is that this respect I had for those I worked with fostered trust. So when I asked for something to be done, the workers were willing to help because they trusted that I had their best interests at heart. In turn, they gave me the benefit of the doubt. So while I had at times an awkward way of managing, they returned the respect I gave them because I always treated them fairly and as equals."

With trust and respect, others will give you the benefit of the doubt. Without trust and respect, motivational techniques come across as manipulation.

"So what can I do to bring more Ubuntu into my department?"

"That is the simplest part. You begin by recognizing

the humanity, the equality, and the value of each person. You accept their humanity without condition. That is, you trust and respect every employee for who they *are*, not for what they have done or not done."

> **ubuntu!**
>
> **Ubuntu starts with recognizing and embracing the humanity, the equality, and the value of each person.**

"But what if giving others such respect does not result in the performance I expect?"

"There will be those who really don't want to do the work they are being asked to do but are afraid of the consequences if they don't. It eventually will be your job to help them find something they will enjoy doing. That may require that they find another job or career path, but that is not the beginning of the story, it is the end."

"Okay. But there is something I'm unclear about."

"What is that, Boss?"

"What if I don't feel the respect for others you talk about? Do I fake it?"

"There are those who advocate that route. For me, I think this is bad advice. Faking doesn't work; you cannot build trust with dishonesty. Each of us can detect a phony. You can't just *do* Ubuntu. You must find a way to *be* Ubuntu."

"And how do we be Ubuntu? What exactly does Ubuntu look like at work?"

ubuntu!

You can't just *do* Ubuntu.
You have to *be* Ubuntu.

"The first step is to get to know your employees as people and not just as workers. That involves developing a sincere interest in each person. What is important to them? Do they have a family? What life experiences have shaped who they are? What are their interests? What are their goals? Where do they hope to be in five years? Are there hot buttons or things they would respond negatively to because of their past that you need to know in order to best work with them?"

"What if they don't tell me about themselves? What if they don't want me to get to know them?"

"What do you think would be the respectful response?"

"Backing off?"

"Yes. You must respect their wishes."

"And those who are not performing? Do I need to treat them respectfully as well?"

"You do not have to respect sloppy work, a bad attitude, or missed deadlines, but you do have to always be respectful of the person who does the bad work even as you work to improve it."

"Simon, my head is spinning. What you are saying makes sense, but I recognize that it is a long way from how I have managed my staff in the past and how I have lived my life. While I have fleeting glimpses of what it might be like to manage this way, it is a bit overwhelming. I want to give it a try, however. Thank you, Simon."

> **ubuntu!**
>
> **Ubuntu does not mean respecting bad work;
> it does mean respecting the person who does
> the work.**

Tuesday Morning

32   T HE THREE-DAY holiday weekend seemed to have taken its toll on John's team. The people in his department seemed moody and sluggish. John had steeled himself for his early-morning meeting with Nancy, only to have Nancy's secretary call to reschedule for Friday. Friday, not a good sign. They let people go on Friday.

In the meantime, John was determined to give Ubuntu a try. He thought about it all weekend. He hung around the break room trying to start a conversation about the weekend with several employees but had little luck. His staff all seemed wary of him. He stopped by Ricardo's office to chat, but Ricardo waved him off, saying he had too much work to do. His comment triggered familiar feelings of anger in John.

"I spent part of my weekend doing the work all of you didn't do properly last week. And now you tell me you have 'too much work'?"

Ricardo looked down at his desk sullenly and said

nothing. John left his office steaming. After a few more halfhearted attempts at employing Ubuntu with his staff, he questioned the wisdom of the whole idea.

The Meeting John Feared

O N FRIDAY, he reported to Nancy's office for their scheduled meeting. Nancy began by exchanging pleasantries for a few minutes, asking about the condition of John's dad. But then it was time for the difficult part of the conversation, and John found himself sweating. Nancy's next statement didn't make him feel any more at ease.

"John, you have always been a hard worker. I want to put your mind at rest right now. With the quality of your work there will always be a job for you while I am here. But it may not be as a manager."

"But you just said I am a hard worker."

"You are one of the hardest workers I know. But we are not paying you to be the hardest worker. We pay you to be an effective manager and leader of a team. Something is wrong when you have to stay late and come in on weekends to meet your department's obligations, doing or redoing your people's work."

"I don't like to do that, either, Nancy. But I don't know what else to do. I'm understaffed and not getting the kind of high-quality work from my staff that I need," John said defensively. "No. Let me correct that. I am not getting high-quality work from anyone except Simon and one other coworker, Nicole."

"That is the point, John. I am happy to hear about Simon and Nicole. Your managerial leadership may not be as deficient as I thought. But it is bad. Surely this is no surprise to you, John. Your past supervisors have told you something very much along the lines of what I am saying."

"My results have always been satisfactory, if somewhat late. And my career development guidelines only include the suggestion that I attend managerial seminars, most of which are taught by young trainers with little or no management experience."

"Do you remember the gist of any of those management seminars?"

"Sure. 'Being a manager is different from being an individual contributor.' Or 'You have to be nice to your employees.' Look, Nancy, I want to be a better manager. But present circumstances force me to redo a lot of the technical work in order to get the job done. I'm barely keeping my head above water."

"And how long has it been like this?"

Once again, John was visibly deflated. "It feels like it's always been like this for me, since I have been in this position."

"John, I know this isn't a good time for you personally, but I believe it is important for me to act swiftly when there is an issue that affects performance. Perhaps you weren't cut out to be a manager, after all. You are welcome to have your old technical job back if you don't want to work with the people you are supervising. It would of course have to be in another part of the company. Or you can try to solve the problems in your department in a reasonable period of time, say, ninety days. I'll leave the choice to you."

"I want to solve the problem and keep my current job."

Nancy looked skeptical. "And when will you be ready to talk about how you intend to solve the problem?"

"Actually, I have a few ideas." He told Nancy about his day with Simon and the concept called Ubuntu. He also shared his early failures and his doubts.

"John. I'll be honest here. I wasn't expecting this. But you are leaving me with a sliver of hope. I think you have started on the right path—I encourage you to pursue this direction. The fact that you are being honest with yourself about your shortcomings is a good sign. You are fortunate to have Simon on your staff. It reflects well on you that you hired him and, better yet, that you are engaging with him. But changing how you manage your department is not going to be easy. And I hope it's not too late.

"The deadline stands: You've got ninety days to show me you can handle this job as a top-notch manager and turn things around. I wish you the best. But I want you to leave here knowing that you need to solve this problem. You will either succeed as manager or be moved to a technical role. Let's schedule a time to touch base on your progress in a couple weeks."

"Will do, Nancy."

"Your comments about Simon are timely. I just learned that Simon is one of the finalists for the grand prize in the OPM contest. He is already a winner of one of the prizes."

"That's great. He is a bright young man, and he deserves the recognition." *Where did that come from?* John wondered.

"He will be asked to attend a corporate event, and managers are requested to join the winners if at all possible. Here are the details. I am going to take a risk here; I hope it doesn't come back to haunt me. I think, especially given what we have discussed, that you should go with Simon and participate in the awards ceremony. Perhaps lend Simon some support. Does that work for you?"

"I would be delighted to support Simon."

Simon and John Revisit Ubuntu

A FTER HIS meeting with Nancy, John was eager to continue his discussion with Simon. The following Wednesday he stopped at Simon's desk and invited him to lunch. He took Simon to a place called Serious Meat.

After their meal was served and they had talked about the OPM contest, John said, "Simon, I was encouraged by our discussion a week ago. But I became discouraged when I tried to put the ideas of Ubuntu into practice. In fact, I lost my temper with Ricardo. How can I use Ubuntu to become a better manager? So far, my efforts have backfired."

Visibly uncomfortable, Simon looked down and said, "It's not my place to tell you how to manage, Boss. I am not an expert; I am just a student."

"I don't want to make you uncomfortable, Simon.

But by helping me see another way to manage, you are contributing to the greater good of the department—and to my career. So helping me is Ubuntu. Right?"

Simon smiled. "You've got me, Boss."

"My journey started," Simon began, "with being open to feedback from my employees. For example, I had one older woman who worked for me who once asked if she could give me some personal advice. Since I've never had an employee request that before, of course I said yes. She pointed out that when I was upset with people, I let my frustration and my emotions get the best of me. And it made it more difficult for others to hear what I had to say. I had lost sight of my goal—to get the other employees to work more efficiently. So I learned to wait until I was calm and collected before discussing a problem with an employee so we could focus on what could be done, not what had been done."

"What a great story. I'm surprised she had the courage to speak up."

"That is a part of the Ubuntu tradition. When someone in a village is acting in a way that threatens the harmony and unity of the community, the elders take action. Ubuntu is a compassionate philosophy, but it is not soft. My temper was threatening the harmony of the community, and the woman, as an elder, felt the responsibility to tell me so."

"Have you ever had a manager who practiced Ubuntu, Simon?"

"Yes."

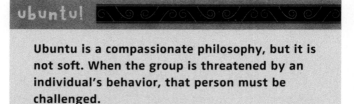

Ubuntu is a compassionate philosophy, but it is not soft. When the group is threatened by an individual's behavior, that person must be challenged.

"What was he or she like?"

"He always treated me as if I were important even when I made a mistake. He was focused but fair. He treated me with respect. And he encouraged me and challenged me to grow. He was fun to work with because he didn't act as if he were better than me even though he knew many things I did not know. My father treated me in much the same way."

Simon continued, "Do you think that you manage in a way that is consistent with your beliefs about people?"

"I believe that when you take a job and get paid a salary, you owe the company a full day's work. I guess I don't feel I should need to beg employees to do the job they were hired to do. I'm not a baby-sitter, after all."

"Yes, but you are a coach and a leader. Those under you look to you for guidance and direction. They work better when they know you care about them."

"Hmm. That's a good point. But I find too many employees feel they are owed something just for showing up. You are an exception, Simon."

"And how did you find out I was an 'exception,' as you call it?"

"Well . . . Well, I got to know you, I guess."

"That is exactly my point. Have you taken time to get to know your other employees?'

It was John's turn to show discomfort. "I guess I really haven't done that."

"So your disillusionment about people is so strong that it affects how you act and behave around your staff. You create a world that fits your beliefs. John, my point is that many of us who work under you might be giving you what you expect to get, in part because you have not taken the time to get to know them—to give them a chance to be on your side. They don't know you. All they know is that you are the boss and they must do as you say. Once you let differences define your relationship with them, instead of the things you have in common, it creates a situation of you against them. So you push against them, and they naturally resist. You then have to rely on the authority of your position to get something done your way. At the core, you have formed no human connection, no reason for them to care."

"But don't they have to earn my trust?" John protested.

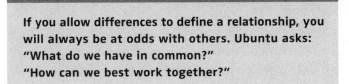

If you allow differences to define a relationship, you will always be at odds with others. Ubuntu asks:
"What do we have in common?"
"How can we best work together?"

39

"Apparently so," Simon answered, again looking down.

There was another pause as John reflected on what Simon had told him. Finally, John spoke again, still resisting: "It just doesn't seem fair."

"What doesn't?"

"I've worked hard to get to where I am. I *earned* my position as a manager. And now I might lose it because of them."

"Yes," Simon agreed, "you work very hard. Perhaps much harder than you would have to work if you had a team working with you. You have earned the opportunity to be a manager of other people. But now you must learn to manage them. We spent a Saturday together because the team's work was not finished, and you and I did what was necessary to get it done. I think you have trained your staff to count on you. How often do you work late to cover for the shortfall by your team?"

"Too often. And now I'm on probation."

"Probation? I didn't know."

"Nancy has given me three months to turn the department around. I am not sure where to start. That is one reason I asked you to lunch. I could use any advice you might have about using Ubuntu to be a better manager. Both Nancy and I feel Ubuntu—or something like it—may be what we need."

"Okay. Well, you might begin by adopting a new approach. Think about every member of the team as someone you want to have succeed. We each have hopes, fears, strengths, weaknesses, dreams, and doubts.

"The people in a rural village in Africa support one another because it is for the common good. In a big company with a hierarchy, we can lose sight of our common bond. If you want to bring Ubuntu alive at work, you may need to start with your attitude and beliefs about people."

"I did try engaging the staff after our last discussion, but it did not go well. It felt awkward and forced, and the employees I approached pushed me away."

"Did you believe in what you were doing? Did you care about them as people? Or were you simply going through the motions without really believing in what you were doing?"

"I guess I was doing what I thought was expected of me. But how can I believe in something I have never tried before?"

"How do you expect your team to take what you do seriously if you are unsure of yourself? Especially now, when you are trying to change your current relationship with them."

"What do you suggest?"

"Find a way to honor the human connection you have to others."

"It sounds easy. But some of my staff seem totally disengaged; a few even seem to dislike me."

"In my experience, Boss, the longer someone has been disengaged from their work, the longer it is likely to take

41

to get them to be an active contributor. Patience is required—as well as persistence. But I believe it is worth the effort. And frankly, Boss, what choice do you have?"

"I see your point. My way of managing my people has not served me very well. But I worry about whether I can change."

"In saying so, you already have changed." Simon beamed.

Startled by Simon's comment, John realized it was true. "I guess I have started to change. I certainly wouldn't have been able to have this conversation a few weeks ago. I am determined to find something positive about my staff that I can believe in and build from there. That will be my strategy."

"That's good, Boss. And remember that Ubuntu is about all of life, not just about work."

"I hadn't thought of that. Perhaps I can bring Ubuntu into what is left of my family life, too."

"People are people, wherever you find them."

John thought of his wife and daughter and how much he missed them. *I wonder if I can repair my relationship with my wife.* It was not just the amount of time spent at work, he realized. *When I was home, I was not much of a partner or father. But we did have something once. Perhaps . . .*

Simon cleared his throat.

"Sorry, Simon. I drifted away for a moment there."

"Tell me about your family."

So John told Simon his story.

John Looks for Something in Which He Can Believe

As JOHN drove home to his tiny rented studio apartment, his mind dwelled on what it was that he believed in regarding the people under him. The more he thought, the clearer it became to him that he really didn't believe his team could change, and so he couldn't start there. He popped a CD into the car's sound system; as his favorite music filled the car, he let his mind wander. He pictured the orchestra playing and let the music fill his head. Suddenly he realized how he could begin to remake himself at work.

43

Ubuntu must begin with me. I believe I can change.

On arriving home, John picked up the phone and dialed a number he knew like the back of his hand. His ten-year old daughter, Beth, answered.

"Hi, sweetheart, it's Daddy. How was school today?"

"Bobby pulled my hair."

"That must have hurt. Did you report him to the teacher?"

"Daaad. I think he likes me."

"Oh."

"Mom wants to talk to you. Love you."

"Love you, too."

"Hello, John. We need to decide when you will see Beth this weekend. It isn't fair to keep her hanging."

"What would you suggest, Alice?"

"Excuse me?"

"What works best for the two of you? I just want to be sensitive to your schedule."

"Well, that's a first," Alice said.

"I'm sorry, Alice. I realize what I have put you through. But I want to change. And I believe I can change. Today is a new beginning for me. I want to be sensitive to your needs. So what works best for you?"

Not accustomed to that kind of exchange with her husband, Alice got right to the point. "Well, it would be best for us if you took Beth on Saturday; I wanted to take her to see Mom and Dad on Sunday. Okay?"

"Great. I thought I would take Beth on a picnic to Grayson's Park. Can I pick her up at ten?"

"Yes, that would be fine—she'll be ready."

"Umm, Alice—can you join us?"

"Oh, John, I don't think I am ready for that."

"I understand. But it would be nice if you decided to come. I would like that."

"I don't think so. Beth has something else she wants to say, so I will give her the phone now."

"Alice."

"Yes."

"I know I have been a jerk. I am sorry."

"Yes. Well. Good-bye, John. Here is Beth."

John Tries Again at Work

To bring Ubuntu into his managerial actions at work, John began by taking small steps. He looked for opportunities to show he cared about his employees for who they were. Rather than hang around the break room, forcing himself on his staff, he waited for opportunities to emerge naturally. As he talked with members of his staff, he began to think constantly about the principles of Ubuntu and look for ways to connect with those around him.

Rather than tackle the most difficult relationships among his staff, such as his relationship with Ricardo, he focused on helping those who already were doing good work and with whom he had a reasonable rapport. Each day he reminded himself that every member of his team had a story. He began to listen to some of those stories; occasionally he had a chance to share a small part of his own story.

45

John thought about trying to approach his relationship with his wife, Alice, in a similar fashion. He began spending more time with his daughter. When he and Alice crossed paths, he took pains to listen to her in a way that allowed him to see the world through her eyes.

A week later, he asked Alice to join Beth and him for dinner at their favorite Italian restaurant, and he was surprised when she accepted. Over dinner, she asked him about work, and he told her and Beth about Simon. His conversations with Simon, he told her, had led him to take a closer look at himself—and he didn't always like what he saw. But he was determined to change. When they parted company that night, there seemed to be a slightly different tenor to their relationship. It was as if a window had been opened, if only a crack. The last thing Alice said to him was, "I would like to meet Simon. He sounds lovely."

Our People Matter
Awards Ceremony

JOHN AND Simon took the back roads from Barrington to Shaumberg, across the massive traffic jam on the freeway. There were only a few people in the auditorium when they arrived. They took seats in the front row.

The BullsEye Auditorium was about half full when Steve Christensen arrived. Not bad for a Friday in July, he thought. He looked around the room for Rolando, who was scheduled to be back from vacation. The vice president of human resources for BullsEye, Sylvana Muchado, mounted the stage, announcing the beginning of the short program. Steve quickly took a seat.

"May I have your attention, please. I am Sylvana Muchado, and I am here today to announce the winners of the Our People Matter contest, or OPM, as we refer to it. First, I want to thank all who participated here in Schaumburg, over on the Barrington campus, and at BullsEye locations around the world." Sylvana went on to talk about the goals of the Our People Matter initiative and the role she hoped it would play in inspiring BullsEye employees and showing them how much they mattered to BullsEye's success in achieving its financial and customer goals.

"My job today is to announce the grand prize winners in the Our People Matter contest. Assisting me today is the chief operating officer of BullsEye, Scott Davis."

Scott loped onto the stage with the vigorous energy of an executive always aware that others are watching him.

A round of applause greeted him.

"Earlier this week a team of volunteers selected five winners from the over 2,500 participants who entered the Our People Matter contest. Let's give everyone a hand for their participation and the hard work they put into writing these essays."

Another round of applause ensued.

"The three envelopes I have in my hand," Sylvana said, "contain the grand prize winners and the runners-up. Scott, here are the third place winners. Would you please open the envelope and make the announcement."

Scott took the envelope containing the two third place winners and opened it. He said, "The winners of a thirty-six-inch flat-screen TV are . . . Connie Nelson from our Minneapolis store and regional warehouse and Robert Newsome from the Denver store. I hope you two are watching on our BullsEye satellite network. Your prizes will be on the way to you today. Let's give Connie and Robert a hand."

"Okay, Scott. So tell us who won the digital surround sound system and media center, complete with installation."

Scott opened the second envelope and said, "Our second place winner is Ian Thorpe from our BullsEye megastore in Sydney, Australia. Congratulations, Ian. What time is it in Sydney, Sylvana?"

Sylvana looked uncertain, but someone in the audience shouted out, "One in the morning on Saturday."

Sylvana quickly added, "Well, Ian, even though you probably are not at work at this hour, never fear, we will send you both the prize and a copy of the award ceremony video so you can share it with your highly motivated team in Sydney. Let's give Ian a hand."

After more polite applause, Sylvana went on. "And now the moment you have all been waiting for so patiently. Scott, why don't you announce the two grand prize winners. Who are the winners of the trip of a lifetime?"

Scott leaned to the microphone. "The first grand prize winner is Stephan, wait a minute, Stephen Christensen of our own headquarters staff."

Steve felt a jolt of electricity course through him.

"Stephen, are you out there?"

A popular member of the headquarters staff for over twelve years, Steve was greeted with strong applause and a number of whistles.

"And from our Barrington office, the winner is . . . Simon Mogutu. Simon, if you are here, please join Stephen on the stage."

Simon rose in astonishment, a deer in headlights look on his face. He headed for the stairs leading up to the stage.

"Come on up, Simon. We have a surprise for both of you."

Stephen walked out on stage and shook hands with the executives as Simon made his way onto the stage.

Scott gave the microphone back to Sylvana, who said, "Well done, Stephen and Simon. And now for the fun part. As you are already aware, you have won a trip to Africa. Some of you are wondering how we could spend BullsEye resources on a trip to Africa during these soft economic times. The answer is simple; this trip is sponsored by our travel partner, Flyaway Airlines, with which we do a lot of business.

"Each year Flyaway chooses one of its corporate customers and supplies that customer with a half dozen tickets to one of its many worldwide destinations. Because our use of Flyaway increased dramatically last year with the opening of our regional office and data center in Atlanta, they have selected us for this honor. Rod Steensland, VP of marketing from Flyaway, is here in the audience. Rod, stand up and let us show our appreciation. Thanks, Rod.

"Yes, you heard me correctly—Flyaway is supplying us with half a dozen tickets. You may be wondering how the other four tickets will be used. Thanks to Flyaway's generosity, both of you will be accompanied by your manager and a family member, friend, or person of your choice."

There were a few gasps and a thunderous round of applause.

"Who is your manager, Steve?"

Steve pretended to look confused, "You mean my boss? Last time I checked, it was Kathy Carter."

"Kathy, would you come up?"

"And Simon, who is your manager?"

Simon just stared into space.

"Simon, I can see you are a bit overwhelmed. Is your manager with you today?"

Simon looked down at John in the front row and said, "John Peterson."

"John. Please join us on the stage. Kathy and John, congratulations. You are lucky enough to supervise an OPM winner, and as such you will accompany Steve and Simon on a safari and on a tour of Johannesburg, South Africa. What do you think about that?"

Kathy leaned toward the microphone, "As a woman of African descent, Sylvana, I have always dreamed of traveling to my homeland. I am simply . . . overwhelmed. Thanks for being a valued employee, Steve, and for working so hard on OPM. I am extremely grateful for the opportunity we had together." She extended her hand to Steve.

As he took her hand, Steve thought of the unkind things he occasionally said about Kathy. But he smiled politely and shook her hand and gave her a half hug.

"And John. What do you think about this adventure?"

"Well, I'm concerned about getting our work done, of course, but it is an extraordinary opportunity. It will give me a chance to see firsthand an African philosophy Simon recently introduced me to. I want to thank Simon."

Sylvana offered a well-practiced smile. "Another great BullsEye employee worrying about how the work will get done. As I noted earlier, Simon and Stephen will each be allowed to bring a guest."

Sylvana looked at Steve. "How about that, Steve?"

"Great, just great, Sylvana."

"And who will you ask, Steve? Do you have someone special in your life? "

The room quieted when the HR executive asked Steve her seemingly innocuous question. Many present knew that Steve's fiancée had died a year earlier, just weeks before their wedding. There was some nervous rustling among the audience. But Steve responded with aplomb. "I don't have anyone special in my life at the moment. So I would like to invite my colleague and friend Rolando Garcia. It was Rolando who encouraged me to enter the contest. He's just back from vacation, but I won't hold that against him if BullsEye doesn't."

Steve heard polite laughter laced with relief.

Sylvana, unaware of the underlying dynamics, said, "Excellent, and we look forward to your presentation to the company, right here in this auditorium, soon after you return. I probably should have mentioned that there is a free trip but no free lunch. The winners and their managers will be asked to share something that they learn on this trip that will help make BullsEye a better place to work.

"Simon, how about you? Who would you like to invite?"

Simon looked off into the distance.

"Simon?"

"This is all very confusing," Simon finally said. "Africa

is my homeland. I am from South Africa, and my wife is from the Congo. I would like to invite my wife. But we are here on visas, and I need to see if that is possible. And we each have our jobs here."

"We will have the HR department help with your visa questions, Simon. But trust me, the work will get done. You won't be gone that long! Let's give all the winners a hand."

The Coffee Shop Across from BullsEye Headquarters

52   STEVE LOOKED sheepishly at Rolando. "You don't have to go if you don't want to, Rolando. Sylvana called me later and apologized. Someone told her about my situation; she was genuinely upset at herself. She said that as VP of HR she lives in a glass house. So what do you think? Will your wife let you go?"

"I am honored to be asked, my friend, and I know Jenny will be excited for me to have this experience. Yes, I would love to come. Do you know what is expected of us when we return?"

"No. The first I heard of that was at the awards. But I'm sure we can whip something together; we always do."

"It sounds like an incredible trip."

The Car Ride Back to Barrington

STILL IN shock, Simon?" John asked.
"I am. Sylvana offered to help me with any visa

problems we have, but I think that my wife will not be able to go. She is from the Congo; her visa has different conditions than mine. It is complicated."

"How about you?"

"That should not be a problem. South Africa and the U.S. have good relations. But how can I go back to Africa and not visit my family?"

"Maybe you will, Simon. It can't hurt to ask. You are the winner, after all."

"Is the trip going to be a problem for you, John?"

"I will need to talk with Nancy. Frankly, she may not let me participate while I am on probation."

"We don't leave until after the July Fourth weekend. Perhaps by then . . ."

53

The African Trip Winners Meet

THE BULLSEYE African trip winners decided to get together to introduce themselves to one another over Sunday brunch on the day after the July Fourth holiday. Kathy brought her husband, Mark, and Simon brought his wife, Sarah. As Simon had feared, his wife would not be able to leave the United States without jeopardizing her visa status. He had called Sylvana and told her about his problem. She told him not to worry; she would take care of it so that the ticket from Flyaway was not wasted.

John had discussed the trip with Nancy and was shocked when she gave him permission to go. She said she believed the African opportunity was quite timely, given what John was learning about Ubuntu, and volunteered to see that the department got its work done. John was overcome with emotion.

"John, you are on probation as a supervisor," Nancy told him. "But you are not on probation as an employee or as a person. You are a good person, and I know you have made a major contribution as a BullsEye employee. I have seen your efforts to establish a different kind of relationship with your staff. I know that it has been hard but that you are trying your best. I have no trouble authorizing this trip, especially in light of the relationship you and Simon have developed."

Over brunch, the group discussed dates, logistics, shots, dress, and things to read about Africa. Simon had been helpful with book recommendations; it was clear that Kathy was fascinated with Simon and Sarah.

As they sat sipping their coffee, Kathy said, "Should we talk about our assignment in Africa?"

"Exactly what are we supposed to do?" Steve asked. "Rolando and I weren't real clear on the task."

"Broadly speaking, we are supposed to return to BullsEye with something useful to offer the organization. It might be an idea, a useful bit of information, or a possible solution to a problem facing the organization. The only stipulation is that it have something to do with the theme that people matter. What did you hear, John?"

"In the car ride back to Barrington, Simon brought me up to speed on OPM. I then contacted HR to get more background. BullsEye launched OPM to bring home the point that its people really matter and that when you put people first, motivation and productivity and better customer service follow. He told me about companies that treat employees as their first priority, even ahead of their customers. As you suggest, if we stay close to the theme that people matter, I think we'll be on target.

"Over the last few weeks Simon has been telling me about an amazing African philosophy called Ubuntu. I think there is a clear connection between Ubuntu and the idea that people matter."

"Fascinating," Kathy commented. "I was already excited about my first trip to Africa, but this connection to Ubuntu adds another level of interest."

For the next half hour the group peppered Simon with questions about South Africa and Ubuntu. Sarah explained that in the Congo the concept of Ubuntu had a different name, although it meant essentially the same thing.

As their conversation wound down, Kathy said, "We should have no trouble finding insights that we can bring back to BullsEye."

Mark looked at his wife quizzically. "Kathy, I am at a bit of a loss here, as I don't work at BullsEye. Perhaps the group could bring me up to speed on some of the challenges you face. I thought people had always mattered at BullsEye."

Kathy glanced briefly at Rolando and Steve. "Let's just say that BullsEye is a great place to work in most of the usual categories. It has great benefits. The salaries are competitive. The store discounts are a real savings that other organizations can't match. But it is a big company with big company issues."

"Such as?"

"You are not going to let me off the hook on this are you, Sweetie? All right. The OPM initiative was a result of the all-employee survey. Those results have not been widely disseminated because they were devastating. Employees don't feel respected at the company. Younger employees are dissatisfied and looking for other employment because of difficulties with their managers. In the summary report on employee satisfaction, results were significantly lower than in any previous survey.

"The only positive, if you can call it that, is that our competitors are not doing any better. After the economic recession that cost so many their jobs, our people are feeling fearful and unappreciated. They may put up with their jobs until the economy gets better, but they are not as productive as they could be. And when the opportunity arises, many are likely to leave."

"And if that wasn't enough," Steve said, "our customer satisfaction scores are also lower. Add our lower sales results, and the overall picture isn't pretty. The OPM initiative is a response to the problem. We can't use the recession as an excuse. We need to strengthen our workforce to assure our future."

Rolando looked at Kathy. "Aren't most big organizations having similar problems? People's retirement accounts have lost value. Homes have lost value. Salaries have been frozen, and many have seen their cost of living go up. Many of our employees are hurting financially. But that isn't the fault of BullsEye."

"True, Rolando. But as economic conditions improve, we need to be able to attract, keep, and motivate a top-notch workforce. If we wait until the economic climate is better to begin to address these issues, it will be too late."

"Got it."

"Does anyone have anything they want to add before we head home? Steve?"

"One of the things Rolando and I often discuss is how hard it is to motivate employees, especially the younger workers."

Kathy smiled. "Well, fortunately, you and I have never had any problems in this area. You guys work hard and do a great job." Steve and Rolando looked at each other skeptically. "What?" she asked them.

Steve decided he needed to say something. "Well, Kathy, you really know your stuff . . ."

"But?"

"Sometimes you seem distant and distracted. You almost never compliment us on our work. Like you just did."

"Well, I try to maintain a professional demeanor, if that is what you mean. And I take my job seriously." She glanced at Simon, who was looking uncomfortable.

"'Serious' is a good choice of words, Kathy—it describes your outlook," Steve went on. "And I think work is a little less fun because of it."

"I, I. Oh." And then Kathy sat silently for a moment.

John realized, I might not be the only one on this trip with issues to resolve.

Kathy took a deep breath. "You guys *must* know how I feel. I brag about my team all the time. I am well aware that I can be successful only if you are successful."

Steve and Rolando looked back at her silently, clearly disagreeing. Mark could see the stress lines on his wife's brow.

"So perhaps I have become a bit too serious at work?" she ventured.

They both smiled, and the tension dissolved. Mark took advantage of the break in the conversation to note the long line of people waiting for a table. With that, they said their good-byes.

Part Two

Discovering Wisdom
in Africa

O'Hare Airport

Four days later the group of managers, winners, and
their guests boarded a Flyaway flight for Atlanta, where
they connected to a nonstop flight to Johannesburg.

On the plane, the others met the mystery guest
chosen by Sylvana, Dr. Beth Ann Ling, a professor of
organization behavior, change management, and cross-
cultural communications from Northern Illinois
University. She was a frequent consultant to BullsEye.

They arrived in Johannesburg some twenty-six
hours later. They passed through immigration feeling

like zombies. In the van they quickly decided that sleep was their first priority. At the hotel they went their separate ways, deciding to meet for breakfast at 9 A.M. the following morning.

The next morning, after a quiet breakfast, their bags were collected, and the group headed outside the hotel, where their van waited to take them on the first leg of their African adventure.

Bakubung Lodge and Pilanesberg National Game Park

JOHN SAT behind the driver's seat. Later he realized how fortunate that was, as Karl, the driver, and his partner, Bretta, talked constantly, spewing information about South African lore.

The route to Bakubung Lodge, which was situated next to the Pilanesberg National Park, took them quickly out of Johannesburg and through the South African countryside.

To John, who had spent part of his childhood in Texas and Oklahoma, the landscape varied from the look of Kansas farmland to the more arid soil around Texas's Red River Valley. Karl talked nonstop.

"This is the richest platinum field in the world we are driving through.

"The gold and diamond industries are major employers in South Africa. You have heard of De Beers, I'm sure."

They passed small villages and towns that seemed to have no purpose as well as malls and modern service stations. A shantytown seemed to line the outskirts of each town, large or small.

"Squatters," Karl told them.

"That's not totally true," Simon whispered. "They are simply poor. There is much poverty in the country."

The small tin houses all looked to be the same size, about eight by eight feet. The flat-roofed houses had dirt floors and at least one tire on the roof to protect from lightning and numerous large rocks to hold the roof down in strong winds.

The homes were neatly arranged, if tightly packed. Each shantytown was fenced off and included several hundred homes. Cooking seemed to be done outside; many homes had clothes on clotheslines waving in the hot gentle breeze.

The roads and highways had walking paths alongside them, pounded into the red dirt by use rather than by design. The paths were clearly heavily traveled. In the middle of what often seemed to be nowhere, the group encountered hordes of people walking.

At every stop sign they found people begging. Some of the beggars' crude cardboard signs were quite creative:

I AM HUNGRY.

HELP MY FAMOUS HOCKEY TEAM.

MAY JOY BE WITH YOU.

John read the signs silently. One was particularly painful to read. A grandmother leaned against the stop sign, looking quite ill, while a three-year-old boy darted between cars, his little arms high above his head so that the driver of each car could read his sign:

MY GRANDMOTHER IS SICK.

Sometime later, Bretta said, "As you know, our destination is the Pilanesberg National Park. Some 1.4 billion years ago, this area was the site of the second largest volcano in the world. The crater is a 143,000-acre reserve now; the rim of red rocky hills forms the boundary of the park. Within the rim you will find every type of animal you would have found five hundred years ago.

"You will stay at the Bakubung Lodge. Sturdy high-voltage electric wires keep you safe from the animals at night. We are almost there. That large building on the hill is a casino that sits on the far side of the park from where you are staying. Karl and I are going on holiday there until it is time to take you back, so if you have an emergency, please call."

Rolando joked, "So if we get stepped on by an elephant we can call you?"

Bretta smiled. "In that case, there would be no reason to call."

Kathy and Beth joined in the laughter from the backseat. John remained quiet. The poverty he'd seen outside his window on the three-hour bus trip had overwhelmed him.

Large signs told visitors about dangerous high-voltage wires and about the even more dangerous animals. Are there signs posted on the other side of the fence warning the animals about the humans? John wondered.

They arrived in time for the Friday night feast. After

a quick trip to their rooms, they joined in. Two lambs and a pig were being roasted out in the open on electric spits. A large table was set under the stars, and as it grew dark, candles were lit. The view of the hills was breathtaking. As the air turned cool, John heard someone in their group say, "We are in Africa."

Kathy looked over and said, "Yes, we are in Africa." There was moisture in her eyes. John wondered how much more deeply he would be moved by this experience if he could trace his roots to Africa. There was little talk after that as they all ate heartily.

Since they had arrived, Simon had talked with John about the poverty they had seen on the drive. John was interested in the reaction of the others. "It was such a stark contrast to what we call poverty in the U.S., I felt profoundly sad. Yet in the midst of all that poverty, I also saw people laughing, playing, working. I wanted to do something to help and immediately felt overwhelmed by the thought."

Kathy nodded. "I have seen pictures of the shantytowns before, but the reality was overpowering. The comparison to our own abundance is disquieting. Perhaps there is something we can do. If we take something away from this trip, perhaps we should give something back."

"I agree," John said. And the others, who had been following their exchange, nodded.

Kathy, Rolando, and Steve, exhausted by the journey, decided to retire. But John, Simon, and Dr. Ling remained at the table over coffee. There was something unfinished about the group's previous conversation. John gave it voice.

"I traveled to Mexico for spring break when I was younger, and in college I had a weeklong international experience in England, but I really don't know anything about the world. I watch the news and see the pictures from far-off places, but the reality of being present in this place is a whole different experience. All I can think about is how lucky I am to have been born into the circumstances I was. Many of those we saw seemed so happy, yet they had so little."

"They had little in the way of material goods, but perhaps they had something else that money can't buy," Dr. Ling said. "Given your experience in the U.S., Simon, how do you feel as you think back to your life in Africa?"

"The thing that amazes me the most is how little gratitude people seem to feel for the abundance they have. Rather than be grateful for what they have, so many of the people I have encountered seem to focus on what they don't have."

Beth Ling agreed. "It is hard to feel happy in a world where all you see is what you lack. That is the value of real travel."

"Real travel?"

"Travel that puts you among the people, that lets you see how others live and experience life, as opposed to seeing the world from a cruise ship. Well, I'm ready for bed."

"Good night."

And so they all made their way along the dark paths to their cottages, their minds full of thoughts and images of Africa.

An African Bush Drive

THE GROUP decided to explore on their own the next day and then take a late afternoon bush drive together. At 3 P.M. they met in front of the open-air bush vehicle. Flick, their guide, proved to be extremely knowledgeable about the animals in the reserve and where to find them. By the time they returned, they had seen elephants, baboons, a white rhinoceros, blue wildebeest, zebra, bushbuck, giraffes, lions, red hartebeest, monkeys, ostriches, and more.

To John, the elephants were the most exciting of the animals they saw. They found two males eating the small branches of leaves on the trees along the road. Their guide recognized the elephants by name. The young male was named Baboo; he was hanging out with an older bull, Nugo, who had a broken tusk. Baboo was probably twelve years old; Flick identified him by his size and a torn right ear. At twelve, Baboo was too old to live with a herd.

Flick never missed an opportunity to comment on the obscure details of the sex life of each animal the group encountered. But he also had a more thoughtful side. Kathy, Mark, Steve, and the others were talking about survival in the animal world when Flick spontaneously recited a favorite quote from Robert G. Ingersoll.

———

THERE ARE IN NATURE NEITHER REWARDS
NOR PUNISHMENTS. THERE ARE ONLY
CONSEQUENCES.

———

"That is thought-provoking," Kathy said, expecting a longer discussion on the topic. But Flick quickly reverted to his favorite subject.

Later, on the way back, the group spotted three lions moving gracefully through tall lion-colored grass. Flick thought they might be from the same litter because they were about the same age; there were two males and one female. During the remainder of the trip, Flick dispensed more of his knowledge of the wild.

"Bushbuck disperse when they are frightened and then find each other again by the black markings around their tails. Pregnant females can hold back birth by as much as two months; they like their young to be born during the rainy season so that the birth smell is washed away. They are prey to so many other animals that the young have to be able to run minutes after birth." He called them the McDonald's, or fast food, of the bush.

"The rhinoceros has no natural enemies. They control their own birth rate.

"The monkeys and baboons spend their days up in the hills but come down to the more open valley to spend the night to avoid the pythons and leopards in the hills."

That night, each member of the group slept well.

Dinner under the Stars

T HE NEXT evening at the lodge, during dinner, there was a commotion on the other side of the fence that protected them from the wildlife in the preserve. After spending two days traveling through the preserve, the BullsEye employees and their guests were glad the fence was there. Spotlights illuminated portions of the field so that diners could see any activity. As if on cue, a family of warthogs passed through the light in single file, snorting as they ambled along.

Kathy, looking away from the warthogs, said, "I can't believe I'm here. What an adventure! I will remember this for the rest of my life."

John jumped up, saying, "I want to try to get a picture of the warthogs to send to my daughter." He jogged toward the fence with his camera in hand.

Beth—Dr. Ling—glanced at Simon and then around the table. "I didn't know John had a family."

Simon responded, "I think it is a painful subject for him."

Steve picked up the spirit of Kathy's earlier comment. "I never thought we would get so close to the elephants. Sitting in the middle of a pod of them was unreal. And when the pride of lions walked across the path not twenty feet in front of the vehicle, I thought I had gone to heaven."

"'Pride,' 'pod'—you have a whole new vocabulary." Rolando laughed.

"I did mention that the lions also caused me to almost pee in my pants."

"I think you skipped that part."

Steve smiled at his friend. "I can also tell the difference between a white and a black rhino by the way it carries its head."

"That will be helpful back at BullsEye!" Kathy jumped in, making them all laugh.

When John returned, he said, "I got a good picture. Take a look." He passed his digital camera around for all to see. "I'll make sure you all get copies. Were you talking about work?"

The word "work" created a slightly more serious atmosphere around the table and prompted Steve to say, "Is this a good time to talk a bit about our project? We are headed back to Johannesburg tomorrow for our last three days in Africa. And I understand that when we return we are expected to have a presentation about something we learned on this trip that will help the folks back at BullsEye."

Perhaps it was the wine or the magic of the shared experience, but Kathy suggested, "Why don't we talk candidly with one another about our life at BullsEye." They all agreed.

Rolando and Steve began, and since they both reported to Kathy, she was a major part of their discussion. In a moment of candor she was reminded that her attitude at work—what she considered being professional—her staff described as cold and distant. She was shocked to discover her nickname in the department—the Ice Queen.

But as a result of Kathy's remarks, Steve and Rolando learned that the younger staff members who worked with them thought they were out of touch.

"Beth, I am sorry I started a discussion that by its nature excludes you."

"Don't worry, Kathy. I do a great deal of consulting work for BullsEye. I think of myself as a kind of partner. And I am interested in what Simon and John have to say."

John accepted the invitation. "This is beginning to feel a little like true confessions, but in fact, the timing is good. I've been having a lot of problems with my department, almost from the time I was made a manager. I'm a hard worker, and I guess I expect everyone else to work as hard as I do. I had ready explanations for the problems in my department: the poor work ethic of the young people on my staff, their lack of motivation, doing only enough to get by. With Simon's help and candid feedback from my boss and colleagues, I've come to recognize that the responsible party turned out to be me. And as I sit here tonight thinking about my wife and a daughter I haven't spent enough time with, I have come to see my responsibility there as well." John's voice cracked, and he could not go on.

Simon reached over and patted him on the shoulder. There was a long silence at the table that Beth broke.

"Simon. Perhaps it is a good time for you to share more about your knowledge of Ubuntu."

Simon told the group about his life in Africa and the philosophy on which much of his life was based. He talked about his father and his influence on his life and what growing up was like in his family.

"Ubuntu is the African philosophy that Nelson Mandela and Desmond Tutu credited when asked how the reconciliation between blacks and whites could occur with so little bloodshed and without retribution. It is simple, they would say. We are all members of the human family, and we must work together to achieve a strong South Africa. These are some of the things John and I have been talking about."

Kathy looked at John and said, "I can see you have had quite an education the last six weeks. It says a lot that you were open to hearing it."

John smiled. "When Simon showed up that weekend to help me catch up on the work, I was astounded. Simon's work had been perfect; there was no reason for him to be there. I think his act of generosity helped me pay attention to what he had to say, as a way to understand why he acted the way he did. His actions could not be explained by my assumptions and beliefs about my staff. I know I have much more to learn. But I am indebted to Simon for setting me on a new path."

Simon seemed embarrassed by all the attention he was getting. Professor Beth smiled and said, "It looks like Africa has a lot it can teach us all."

Soweto, South Africa

THE GROUP nervously anticipated their trip to Soweto, but they agreed that they wanted to have a true African experience there, not one that left them looking out a bus window. With Simon's help, they asked at the hotel about other options. They were told to contact Les, an exceptional tour guide who drove his own minivan to take visitors inside Soweto. It was Les who provided the most memorable moments of a highlight-filled week. The insights from the trip to Soweto became the foundation of their work at BullsEye a few weeks later.

Born in Soweto, Les was familiar with every nook and cranny. He was extremely proud of his African heritage. He frequently told them how hard it was for him to believe the changes of the last twenty years in South Africa.

"I think it will take generations—perhaps until my grandchildren's children come of age—for the African heart to be free of the pain of apartheid." But he was hopeful that the pain would lessen over time.

Les had a five-year-old son. Les taught English in the school system and conducted small tours on the side.

"Mandela says we must forgive; I believe he is right. Anger only festers. It is forgiveness that gives you true freedom."

Johannesburg, or Jo'burg, as it was called, Les told the group, had grown up during the gold rush of the 1800s. Blacks came from all over to work in the mines. They had been reduced more or less to slavery in many regions by taxation and hoped to create a new life. Then the government became concerned about the proximity of blacks to white settlers. The whites felt they were losing control of the city.

The solution the white South African government settled on in 1933 was to evict all blacks from the city forcibly. The government set up a farm for blacks eleven miles from Johannesburg. That was how Soweto was born. It was a township without running water, electricity, roads, shops, or police and little public transportation. Overnight Soweto became home to 40,000 people.

Today, Les told them, Soweto was South Africa's largest city. "Some 600,000 live in an area less than eight square miles in size. It is made up of many different neighborhoods. Some neighborhoods house the affluent; others are impoverished, as in any big city."

The group arrived at Soweto fifteen minutes after leaving their comfortable hotel.

"This is the Hollywood of Soweto," Les said. "We'll start here."

The houses looked modern, clean, and well kept. All had fences with closed gates; often razor wire ran atop the fences, as in Jo'burg. The homes, with small yards, were packed tightly together.

"This is where our doctors and lawyers live," Les proudly announced.

Soon the group was on the edge of a swampy area just outside of Hollywood. Les pulled over to show the group the old mining quarters. They were being refurbished by the government to provide public housing.

"Originally, miners slept in bunk beds with no running water or cooking facilities. When the remodeling is complete, these houses will have running water, two bedrooms, and a kitchen for each family."

Les stopped the minivan on a bluff overlooking row upon row of homes. They created a colorful geometric design to the edge of the horizon.

"The next suburb we will come to is an area where people are waiting for the government housing to be finished."

As they drove through the neighborhood, many of those walking on foot along the red dirt road waved and called out, "Welcome to Soweto."

"My people enjoy visitors. Many say it is safer here than in Jo'burg; I would agree."

The group's next stop was an open area next to a busy intersection. There were numerous white vans parked there. Les told John and Kathy they were unofficial taxis.

To the side of the taxi parking lot was a tin hut. A young boy emerged from it and approached Les's minivan. Les introduced him as Timber Zulu. Timber, Les told them, would be the group's guide for a walk into the neighborhood.

Before them, Steve, Rolando, Simon, and the others could see tin houses and a few green Port-O-Potties scattered about, as far as the eye could see. The red dirt path led somewhat downhill before branching off, winding among the houses. Timber, dressed in a faded Burberry baseball cap, faded blue T-shirt, and shorts and wearing no shoes, pointing out homes in the neighborhood, talking nonstop.

Some houses were painted bright colors. Others had flowers or a stalk or two of corn growing beside them. At most, the doorways were open or had a cloth curtain across them. The neighborhood seemed nearly empty, although the few people on the road were very friendly.

One mother came out with a small child, carrying a bucket. She went to the nearest Port-O-Potty and emptied the bucket. The BullsEye group realized that was how the Port-O-Potties were used: for dumping, not for sitting. The potties were cleaned once a week, Timber told them. Sitting inside one would not be a pleasant experience.

Timber told the group he lived with his grandmother. His mother lived in another city, and he rarely saw her. He did not know who his father was.

"Then listen to your grandmother," Simon told him, kindly.

Timber simply rolled his eyes, shrugging, asking, "Why?"

"Because your grandmother is very wise and full of love."

Timber looked at Simon and said, "How would you know? Your grandmother lives in America."

Simon surprised him when he said, "No, she lives in Pretoria. I grew up in South Africa." Timber's eyes lit up; he remained close to Simon for the rest of the tour.

On the way back, the group stopped at the home of a friend of Timber's. The one-room house reeked of butane. The burner, used for cooking, rested on the dirt floor at the foot of a neatly made bed. The only other furniture in the room was a small refrigerator. Everyone in the group thanked his friend for allowing them into his home with a coin or two, as Timber had anticipated.

The group passed a purple house with a fence; a sign read DAY CARE. Timber called it a kindergarten. "They need books. All the schools need books. If you can send T-shirts and pens for the schoolchildren, it would be helpful. You can send them to Les; he will see that they get to the proper place."

John was struck by the fact that Timber wasn't asking for anything for himself but for the children in the community. It is another example of Ubuntu. We should help—we can create a Project Timber.

At the end of their tour, Timber taught John and the others the African handshake—hello, peace, and love—before saying good-bye. Simon, shaking his hand, gave him a few rand.

As the group drove on to the next stop, Les was visibly excited.

"We are approaching the only street in the world to have two Nobel Prize winners as residents: Nelson Mandela and Archbishop Desmond Tutu."

Ubuntu's Best Known Practitioners

A HIGH GRAY fence marked the home of Desmond Tutu.

"Bishop Tutu still spends time in his home when he

is in the area. Mandela's home was just down the way. He and his first wife, Winnie, lived there; it is very small, with just four rooms. He stayed the first two nights in it when he was released from prison ten years ago, but he needed more privacy. Today he lives elsewhere with his current wife. His Soweto house is now a museum."

As the group paid the small admission fee and went on the tour, Les sat under a tree and chatted with other guides. There were several tour groups crowded in the tiny house.

The walls, shelves, and tables were covered with black and white pictures of Mandela meeting people from around the world. In the small kitchen area the many honorary diplomas Nelson Mandela had received were displayed in the open cabinets. His bed was covered in a tribal feather bedspread. Hung around the room were ceremonial robes given to him by the dignitaries of various countries.

"We Africans live by a philosophy we call Ubuntu," the tour guide told them. "It connects all clans. Because of Ubuntu, Mandela and Tutu did not pursue revenge but reconciliation."

Kathy spoke up. "Surely many wanted revenge after all those years of atrocity?"

"That is true. That is part of the genius of Mandela. His philosophy of reconciliation was built around an idea that existed throughout Africa. Because we are all connected in our humanity, Ubuntu suggests that to harm another person would be to harm yourself. To seek revenge on others would be to hurt yourself. Mandela and

Bishop Tutu helped us understand that Ubuntu meant accepting the humanity of our oppressors even as we detested the years of oppression. We had to unconditionally accept the humanity of each human being."

Around the corner from Mandela's home, Kathy and the others visited the Hector Pieterson Memorial. It was erected in the place where many schoolchildren were killed in 1976 while they engaged in a peaceful demonstration. The world-famous picture of a young boy, Hector, limp in the arms of a man carrying him home, with Hector's younger sister running along beside them, symbolized the terrible tragedy of that day. Many in the BullsEye group recognized the picture, although they didn't know the facts surrounding it.

Their guide provided the details. "The police reported fifty-nine killed, but the truthful number is probably closer to five hundred. The students were peacefully demonstrating against the use of Afrikaans—the 'official' language of South Africa that was established by the Dutch—in their curriculum. Hector was not part of the actual demonstration; he was nearby, watching his friends march. He was killed when the police became overzealous in quashing the demonstration. They terrified residents of the area for weeks, driving around in green patrol cars, shooting at anything that moved. Fear kept families huddled inside their homes—they were even afraid to collect their dead."

The story of the protest was told through blown-up newspaper articles and pictures from news organizations all over the world. Hector's sister, they learned, now in her forties, worked at the memorial. The man in the picture who carried Hector home disappeared, probably never to be heard from again. The police searched desperately for him, though he had done nothing wrong. His family last heard from him in 1978; he was living in Saudi Arabia.

Everyone bought beaded necklaces at the small flea market outside the memorial before continuing their journey.

The last stop of the day was Regina Mundi Church, considered the parliament of Soweto. It was still a very large, active Catholic Church, yet it was still pockmarked with bullet holes—a reminder of times past.

Residents thought it was a safe place to gather to discuss their situation. One night in the 1970s, as the church was filled with what is said to have been five thousand people, the police stormed the church. Many people were injured as they fled. The windows had been replaced, but the bullet marks and the memories remained.

Kathy, Steve, John, Simon, Beth, and Rolando were silent on the ride back to the hotel, lost in their thoughts.

Simon's Surprise

THE NEXT morning, Simon had agreed to meet Kathy early for breakfast. It was a free day for the group to explore Jo'burg. As Simon entered the lobby, he noticed a large group of brightly dressed Africans near the entrance to the restaurant. Someone shrieked, "Simon." It was Simon's family, he realized. Kathy and John, working with the consulate, had arranged the get-together. As Simon hugged his relatives, he wept with joy. After brief introductions—John had a chance to shake hands with Simon's father and mother and two of his siblings—Simon and his family left to catch up on all that had happened since Simon had moved with Sarah to the United States.

Insight in Africa

THAT EVENING, the group came together for one last meal in Africa. Simon's family was on its way back to Pretoria, but the smile on Simon's face remained. A tired silence pervaded the dinner table.

Steve broke in: "I'm amazed that an entire country can share such a sense of community. It's one of the things, I realized over the past week, that is missing from our company: a sense of community and unity of purpose. We're all BullsEye employees, but we don't really see ourselves as a community with a common purpose."

Kathy agreed. "What could we achieve if we were all truly working together at BullsEye?"

"What would it look like to embrace the concept of Ubuntu at BullsEye in everything the company and its employees do?" Beth asked. "What would it feel like?"

"I'm not entirely sure," Steve replied. "But it seems as though we would better relate to each other as human beings rather than just as employees or managers."

"It would be like family," Rolando said.

"Embracing a concept like Ubuntu would involve

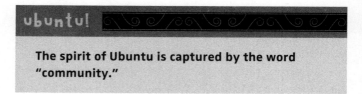

The spirit of Ubuntu is captured by the word "community."

some risks," Kathy added. "But what is the alternative? Continuing to play corporate games, trying more half-hearted initiatives, politics, and gossip, pitting one group against another. Indifference."

"We have too much of that already!" Steve affirmed.

"On the other hand, I believe we have good people," Kathy asserted. "We need to affirm that goodness. Celebrate it. I have come to believe the spirit of Ubuntu lives in each of us. It's more a matter of discovery than of creating something that doesn't exist."

"Agreed," Steve said. And there never was a time when we needed that discovery at BullsEye more than we need it now."

"In the BullsEye of our dreams, a manager would respect the employee as a person even when the employee's work did not at that moment deserve recognition and respect," John observed.

Simon smiled.

"And you have to be honest and direct with your employee, that is, be able to look him or her in the eye and tell the truth," Rolando added.

"And the same would apply to employees," Kathy asserted. "They must be true to themselves and honest and open with their managers."

80

Simon added, "And that honesty does not have to be tactless or lack compassion."

At that moment, Bretta, at a nearby table, interrupted them to tell them she would be driving the group to the airport at 6 A.M. and review the logistics for checking out of the hotel and getting their boarding passes. "I've been eavesdropping on your conversation," she confessed. "I am fascinating by your interest in Ubuntu."

"What do you think?" Kathy asked.

"Steve Biko said that Africa can contribute to the world a more human face. Ubuntu is the core of that message. I think a philosophy as rich as Ubuntu can provoke all kinds of useful ideas and ways of cooperating that can be applied to the workplace. The human spirit is like the dormant grass on the savanna, always waiting to spring to life with the next rain. Too often the human spirit lies dormant below the surface in the workplace. I think of Ubuntu as the rain that can bring it to life.

"But it is odd that you are listening to me talk about Ubuntu. You have an expert in your group."

They each looked at Simon.

Bretta grinned. "Don't you own a business in Pretoria, Simon?"

"My brother and I have a business there."

"And wasn't your business featured in the *Pretoria News* for its unusual business practices?"

"Yes, there was a small article written about it before I went to the U.S."

"A small article. It was on the front page of the Sunday edition! If I remember correctly, you call your business

Ubuntu Manufacturing. You chose that name because of the principles upon which you built your business."

Bretta went on to explain. "Karl and I run a business in Jo'burg. We have a plant in Pretoria, so we are in Pretoria a great deal."

Simon said, "Thank you," his voice almost too soft to hear.

"Front page of the newspaper!" John said as he looked at Simon with admiration. "You left out a few details about yourself, Simon."

"Excuse me," Bretta said, "but I think it is important that your colleagues understand why you are so understated about your success. I guess it is a bit late to ask for your permission, but may I explain?"

Simon nodded.

"Simon doesn't just know about Ubuntu; he lives Ubuntu. And because of that, he will not raise himself above those he works with. Yes, Ubuntu is about the connectedness of people, about unity of purpose. But it is also about human equality. In Ubuntu, managers put ego and self aside. The success of Simon's company isn't about Simon; it's about everyone who works there."

PART THREE

BRINGING UBUNTU HOME

On the Flight Home the Ideas Flow

On the plane back, every seat was taken. Steve, Rolando, and Kathy were seated in one row and John, Simon, and Professor Beth in another. After a meal and a quick catnap, the two groups independently decided to discuss the project.

Kathy posed the question, "If Ubuntu is so highly valued in African society, why isn't it universally practiced there?"

Before long, Steve, Rolando and Kathy were involved in an animated conversation.

"Freedom and equality are highly valued in the United States politically, but they are often not core values within U.S. corporations," Kathy said. Was the same thing true of Ubuntu in Africa?

In the other group, Beth raised a point about recognition and Ubuntu. "It seems to me that the philosophy of Ubuntu frames a kind of recognition that isn't discussed in the management texts or in the corporate training programs. There seem to be two kinds of recognition.

84

"The first is highlighted in the story we heard about how a village treats a stranger. In theory, you could walk across South Africa with only the clothes on your back and never go hungry because each village would offer you food and shelter. Not because you asked or because you were important but because you are a fellow member of the large family we call the human race. This first level of recognition is given unconditionally to every human being. You are respected without preconditions as a member of the human family.

"In the workplace this would mean each person is respected as a person and that respect is not tied to performance. Compassion, honesty, lack of arrogance and self-importance, and a willingness to help others would all be signs of that. Does that make sense to you?"

John responded. "It does make sense. Simon has helped me understand this point. For me to be a better, more effective manager, I need to establish a new relationship with my staff by extending this kind of recognition to all my employees. We are all connected; we are all equal. And we must all help each other and work together as a team. Coaching, performance reviews, feedback, and other management tools are important, but they come second. First comes recogni-   85
tion, the heart of Ubuntu. It helps to breed the trust necessary for everything else that is to follow."

Beth nodded. "And once the first level of recognition is present, the second level of recognition comes into play: rewarding and recognizing others for what they achieve, for their performance and results. You can do it on a formal or informal basis, but it is usually most effective when it is done daily with employees rather than just once a quarter or in an annual review. Does that make sense to you, Simon?"

Simon smiled. "I remember a discussion we had in the class you taught. We were talking about conscious competence and unconscious competence. When I was working in my business in South Africa, I think I was an unconscious competent. My effectiveness came from following the spirit of Ubuntu. Today, thanks to your class and the other classes I have taken, I can describe what I did in business terms. I believe this is one of the things we can take back to BullsEye."

ubuntu!

TWO LEVELS OF RECOGNITION

The first level of recognition is to value others simply for *who they are*. This is the heart of Ubuntu, and it must always come first.

The second level of recognition is to value others for *what they achieve*. This kind of recognition is what drives most performance.

John Discusses His Personal Challenges

I WOULD LIKE to hear more about your challenges as a manager, John, if you are comfortable talking about them," Beth said. "Many of our adult students are managers or are destined to be managers. Almost all of my students work, so if they are not managing, they are being managed. All of them are members of teams, or work in groups or departments of various sizes. I would love to pass along anything I can learn about the challenges of management in the real world in which you live."

"I don't mind, Beth. Your background is psychology, isn't it?"

"Yes."

"Well, it might well be helpful for me to talk about why I haven't been as good a manager as I want to be. I believe I understand what has kept me from being effective as a manager, but I'm not confident I am able to solve the problem. I have interacted with my employees and they have interacted with me in one way for a long time. I made a few attempts to change how I manage before I left, and I was beginning to have some success with some of my staff. But I haven't yet tackled the most challenging members of my team. I'm worried that if I come back acting differently, it will only make them suspicious."

"Tell me more about how you managed before."

"Can I give you a little personal history?"

"We have another ten hours on this plane."

"Well, I am adopted. My adoptive parents adopted five children; we all worked in the family business from the time we were very young. My dad and mom operated a small grocery store in a small town in Minnesota.

"My dad treated us as more of a boss than a dad. I think he had lived under a financial cloud for so long that it made him callous. As a child, I knew he could blow up in anger at any time. And anything that cost money usually led to an outburst. School was my only refuge. But even there I was the butt of a lot of jokes because of the old clothes I wore.

"I worked hard to avoid my dad's anger. I knew he respected hard work. My dad wasn't big on compliments, but I could tell he was pleased with my work ethic. He sometimes called my brothers and sisters lazy, but he never said that about me.

"When I arrived at BullsEye, I was determined to be successful, to be the hardest-working employee in the building. And I carried a lot of my father with me. I kept my head down and just did my work as an analyst, but when I was promoted, my beliefs surfaced and affected everything I did.

"I have assumed most people are lazy, uncommitted, and looking for shortcuts. For example, I didn't realize what a great job Simon was doing until his performance was pointed out by someone else. It forced me to actually see him for the first time.

"To be honest, I am no longer sure I have what it takes to be a good manager. Hard work alone is not enough. I do know there has to be a better way for me to work with my team other than using fear and sarcasm or by doing their work for them when—surprise, surprise—they fail to produce. If I can't figure it out soon, I will lose my job as a manager. So that is my challenge."

"It seems to me, John, that you are in a process of transition. You are letting go of your old ways of managing, but your new practices are evolving. You are in between, and that is a scary and uncertain place to be. To your credit, you have taken a huge step forward; the job is just not yet complete, and that can be unsettling.

Give yourself credit for leaving behind the familiar and comfortable, without a clear path for where to go.

"It's not surprising that you are a bit unsettled and unsure. That is the nature of transition. But the hardest work has already been done, I think. As William Bridges, one of my favorite authors, says, 'a time of transition can be a time of great creativity.' I am confident you will discover everything you need for this part of your journey."

"Thanks, Beth. I'll think about our conversation together. I do believe I feel a sense of hope."

ubuntu!

When you leave what is comfortable and familiar in order to take on something new and exciting, it is natural to feel unsettled and even afraid. This is where the support and collaboration of colleagues is most important.

John Updates Nancy

"How was Africa, John?" Nancy asked at their next meeting together. "Did you have an amazing trip?"

"Yes, in so many ways, Nancy. I know I will look back on the trip to Africa as a highlight of my life. And you were able to get my department to keep up with their work. Did you have any problems?"

"You know the old management saw—any change can be motivating for a while."

In fact, Nancy recognized, John's people seemed to have more energy from the moment he left. But she also could see that at least two of his employees would test any manager's patience. She had some serious discussions with them about their work and attitude. She almost lost her temper with Ricardo.

"Why don't you give me a quick summary, John."

John gave her a ten-minute overview of the trip. Then he talked about what the group had discovered about Ubuntu to help her understand it at a deeper level. "And I learned more about Simon's life as a business owner in Pretoria. Simon may be a first-rate employee here, but he was a respected leader in South Africa."

"Perhaps he is a respected leader here as well."

John smiled and said, "Yes, I believe he is. I had a long conversation with the professor who joined us on the trip about the nature of transitions. It was helpful to see my current situation from the standpoint of transition and change. During the trip I talked to the group about my past. And I have become clearer about why I deal with people the way I do.

"I believe that Ubuntu is a powerful idea that holds answers for me. I know I would like to create the kind of team that only an Ubuntu leader can create. I'm just not sure I know . . ." John paused, overcome by a surge of emotion. "The ways I learned to cope as a child may be too entrenched."

"John, I think what you are saying about old habits

would be true of any of us to some degree. We all have areas we need to grow in, and we all have challenges to meet. For some of us the project lasts a lifetime. In fact, that is part of what makes life so vital. I think you've already answered this, but let me ask you directly. Do you want to change?"

"Yes, I do. I'm just . . . scared, I guess."

"The fact that you are scared, to me, is another sign of progress. You aren't underestimating the size of the challenge. But you may be underestimating the power of the tools you brought back from Africa and the tools available to you here at the office. You may be underestimating your capacity to change. Let's meet again in a few weeks. Are you going to continue to consult with Simon?"

"Yes. Is that all right?"

"Please do. Do you mind if I approve three hours a week in overtime for Simon?"

"Not at all."

"Why don't you let me tell him? I have a feeling he will resist the idea if you suggest it and say that he doesn't expect to get paid for doing what is expected. Ubuntu, right?"

"Right. Thank you."

John's Plan

THAT EVENING, after talking to Alice and his daughter, who of course wanted to know all about the trip, and checking in with his parents and getting an update on his father's progress from his sister, John sat down at the small card table where he ate his meals and opened an unused notebook. He looked at his pictures of his wife and daughter sadly. One thing at a time, he thought. It is time to consider my next steps at work. Bringing himself back to the task at hand, John wrote a headline on the first page and began laying out his plan.

My Guide to Team Development and Building a Community of Purpose

1. It starts with me. My first focus has been and must continue to be the manner in which I behave and manage at work. I must be approachable, open, honest, transparent, supportive, and compassionate. I need to check my ego at the door and act with humility and gratitude.

2. I must build trust by demonstrating my respect for my employees first and only second by focusing on what a person can do. I need to remember that we may have different titles, do different work, and earn different salaries, but at a basic human level we are all the same, and we should treat each other as such. Next, I must follow through on my commitments. My deeds must follow my words.

3. My department is a small community. It has a clear organizational reason for existing. I need to develop a sense of common purpose in my group and explore the ways we depend on one another and others depend on us.

4. I started working on my relationships with my best employees, the low-hanging fruit. I must now focus more on Ricardo and Marta, my two biggest challenges.

5. The conversations between Kathy and Steve made me aware that I am also too serious at work. I need to be able to lighten up and laugh at my own shortcomings and foibles.

6. We spend the largest portion of our life at work. I want to find ways to help improve our quality of life at work.

John next wrote the names of each of his department team members. He tried to visualize each person and thought about what he knew about each one.

The Members of My Work Community

Simon	Scott
Ricardo	Felix
Mia	Nicole
Zhu Zhu	Barbara
Marta	?

What is the name of the tenth member of my team? I have twelve positions; two are vacant. For the life of him, he couldn't remember the name of his tenth employee.

And then, quite suddenly, he started laughing. He laughed about how far he had to go, at the mistakes he had made. He laughed until tears filled his eyes. As he dabbed his eyes with his handkerchief, he looked down at his plan. If I dedicate myself to these steps, I will have given it my best shot. Regardless of the outcome, I will have no regrets.

Team Africa's First Planning Meeting

A WEEK AFTER their return, the six BullsEye travelers to Africa sat comfortably in Conference Room C at BullsEye's headquarters. As the group gathered, there was a constant back-and-forth about the journey they shared, family reactions, the memories they had of the trip, and the insights they had looking back.

"Okay, gang," Kathy finally spoke up. "We have a lot to do in a short time. The first thing we need to accomplish is to decide who will facilitate the meeting. We are equal members on the team. I convened the meeting, but I am not in charge."

Nobody seemed surprised by this statement because Kathy had been open about the changes she wanted to make in her leadership practices. Steve looked around the table and said, "If she is willing, I think Beth would be a great facilitator."

"If that is what the team is in favor of, I am happy to facilitate," Beth responded. The others nodded their agreement. "So let's talk about our assignment and how to approach it."

After about thirty minutes of animated discussion, the group reached a consensus about the next two immediate steps.

"When we talk about making a difference with Ubuntu," John said, "we are implying a change inside the culture of BullsEye. That means we need to be clear about two things: the nature of the change and our strategy to achieve that change. We may decide that the concept of 'Ubuntu' can capture the change we envision, or we may want to elaborate. But I think the vision will be the easy part. The hard part will be clarity about our strategy. We are not implementing a new IT system or a new payroll process. We are not implementing flex hours or telecommuting. What we are trying to bring about requires a personal commitment from everyone in the organization. And that makes it different from the changes we have experienced at BullsEye."

Beth nodded in agreement.

Kathy added, "Steve, Rolando, and I talked about the cynicism many employees have developed about new management or motivation programs. We roll them out with good intentions, but at the individual level it often feels like we roll them over people. People become resistant and detached from these top-down efforts. But if I hear John correctly, the history of such initiatives at BullsEye is only part of the challenge. We want people to bring the Ubuntu philosophy into their lives. And that can never be legislated or mandated."

Beth suggested they brainstorm ways to encourage people to embrace Ubuntu.

John offered a personal observation. "I began to change after being inspired by Simon. He provoked me when he showed up to work on a Saturday, and he inspired me by the way he lived his life at work. I needed both: provocation and inspiration."

Kathy said, "I was provoked by the candor of Steve and Rolando at the brunch before we left for Africa. I was inspired by my experience there and by the conversations we had."

Beth worked feverishly to capture the key ideas on the flip charts. She finally held up her hands in defeat and said, "I need a break. Could we take a time out so I can organize these notes?"

After John brought Beth a cup of coffee, they all headed down to the food court for a snack.

Flip Chart Pages

THE OTHERS knew Beth was good at what she did, but none of them was expecting what they found when they returned. A pile of discarded sheets lay on the floor; only two spare sheets were posted on the wall.

OUR VISION FOR BULLSEYE

<u>WE SEE BULLSEYE AS A WELL RUN AND
PROFITABLE COMPANY THAT IS SEEN BY ITS
EMPLOYEES AS ONE OF THE BEST PLACES
TO WORK, ANYWHERE.</u>

THE UBUNTU PHILOSOPHY AND THE VALUES
IT REPRESENTS CAN GUIDE US TO BECOME:

- A COMPANY WHERE EACH PERSON IS
  TREATED RESPECTFULLY AND WITH DIGNITY

- AN ENVIRONMENT OF FUN AND HARD
  WORK WHERE TEAM MEMBERS COME TO
  ONE ANOTHER'S ASSISTANCE

- A HOME AWAY FROM HOME WHERE
  EVERYONE IS EQUAL AND WHERE EGOS
  ARE REPLACED WITH GRATITUDE AND
  HUMILITY

- A COMMUNITY FROM WHICH EMPLOYEES
  GO HOME AT THE END OF THE DAY WITH
  THE RENEWED ENERGY AND VITALITY THAT
  COMES FROM HARD WORK WELL DONE,
  PRIDE, APPRECIATION, AND A SENSE OF
  ACCOMPLISHMENT

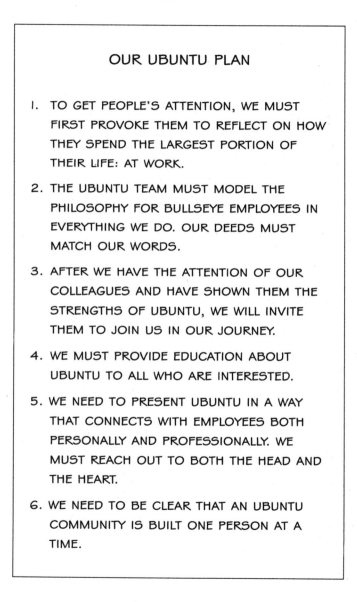

OUR UBUNTU PLAN

I. TO GET PEOPLE'S ATTENTION, WE MUST FIRST PROVOKE THEM TO REFLECT ON HOW THEY SPEND THE LARGEST PORTION OF THEIR LIFE: AT WORK.

2. THE UBUNTU TEAM MUST MODEL THE PHILOSOPHY FOR BULLSEYE EMPLOYEES IN EVERYTHING WE DO. OUR DEEDS MUST MATCH OUR WORDS.

3. AFTER WE HAVE THE ATTENTION OF OUR COLLEAGUES AND HAVE SHOWN THEM THE STRENGTHS OF UBUNTU, WE WILL INVITE THEM TO JOIN US IN OUR JOURNEY.

4. WE MUST PROVIDE EDUCATION ABOUT UBUNTU TO ALL WHO ARE INTERESTED.

5. WE NEED TO PRESENT UBUNTU IN A WAY THAT CONNECTS WITH EMPLOYEES BOTH PERSONALLY AND PROFESSIONALLY. WE MUST REACH OUT TO BOTH THE HEAD AND THE HEART.

6. WE NEED TO BE CLEAR THAT AN UBUNTU COMMUNITY IS BUILT ONE PERSON AT A TIME.

---

7. THE FUEL THAT KEEPS UBUNTU ALIVE
   WILL BE THE ENERGY OF BULLSEYE'S
   EMPLOYEES.

8. THE CENTRAL THEME OF UBUNTU MUST
   BE PRESENT IN EVERYTHING WE DO,
   MAKE, AND SELL.

   <u>WE CAN BE FULLY HUMAN ONLY WHEN WE
   LIVE IN HARMONY WITH OTHERS.</u>

"That's brilliant, Beth," Rolando said. "You have captured the essence of our discussion." He turned to the others and went on. "I have been quiet so far this morning. I have been reflecting on the way I have conducted myself at work. This has led to some genuine soul-searching on my part.

"I believe we're on the right track, but we can do better, we can do more. This whole process, from the preliminary meeting to the trip to Africa and our work here today, has helped me to be truthful with myself. I want to change how I behave at work. I want to work with inspiration, with passion. I don't feel I've been giving the job my best effort. And that, I realize, is unacceptable to me. That is not how I want to spend the bulk of my days. I am sorry, especially to Kathy, who has put up with me for four years."

Kathy looked at Rolando and gave him a big smile. "Rolando, you have always been a solid contributor. If you can do more, I welcome it. We have both had our ups and downs. And I am equally responsible. We all seem to have grown from this experience. As I listen to John and Simon describe their journey, I am reminded of how fortunate we are to be here. Now let's share our good fortune with others and see if we can light a few more fires under our colleagues. Let's make Ubuntu spread like a wildfire.

"By the way, our CEO, Len Dufore, wanted to be here today. He wanted to visibly lend support to what we are doing. But I asked him to let us meet first on our own. I am told he has a personal interest in the project. I agreed to brief the top management team on our progress. If you are all in agreement, I would like to present these two flip charts to them. Perhaps you could all join me when I do and help us prepare by asking the questions that might come up."

Rolando was quick to reply. "I'll start. Kathy. What does Ubuntu look like when you see it in the workplace?"

Kathy opened her mouth to respond to the question but there was no sound. She looked around the table and finally broke the silence by saying, "I can't believe we have missed something so important. Brilliant question Rolando and exactly the sort of thing an executive would ask. But it is also a question that exposes a weakness in our presentation. We have gotten so close to Ubuntu that we have forgotten that people will need examples. We need to provide those examples."

She looked around the table again. "I suggest we deal with this immediately. Can we do this right now? Could you stay a while longer?"

They all nodded.

"Any ideas on how we should procede?"

John leaned forward, "I think we should describe Ubuntu scenes from everyday work life. As I was working with my own issues I would often envision what it would look like to put the principles of Ubuntu into action in real situations."

"I love that John. Lets brainstorm scenes from a work life with Ubuntu. Ubuntu sightings if you will. Later we can ask BullsEye employees to share their Ubuntu sightings."

An hour later flip charts once again covered the wall.

- BEFORE STARTING THE WORKDAY I THINK ABOUT THE THINGS FOR WHICH I AM GRATEFUL. DOING THIS AFFECTS MY ATTITUDE AND I FIND MYSELF MORE POSITIVE DURING THE DAY.

- WHEN SOMEONE IS WALKING TOWARD ME IN THE CORRIDOR I THINK ABOUT HOW I WOULD WANT TO BE GREETED AND PUT ON A SMILE AS THEY APPROACH.

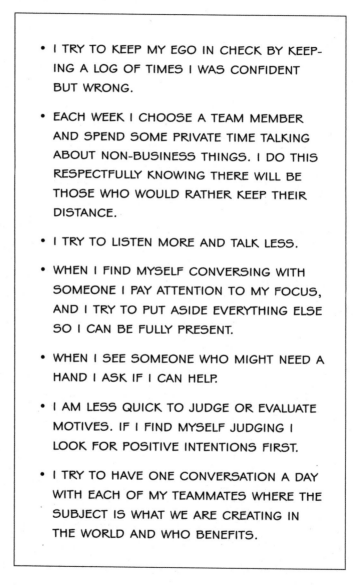

- I TRY TO KEEP MY EGO IN CHECK BY KEEP-
ING A LOG OF TIMES I WAS CONFIDENT
BUT WRONG.

- EACH WEEK I CHOOSE A TEAM MEMBER
AND SPEND SOME PRIVATE TIME TALKING
ABOUT NON-BUSINESS THINGS. I DO THIS
RESPECTFULLY KNOWING THERE WILL BE
THOSE WHO WOULD RATHER KEEP THEIR
DISTANCE.

- I TRY TO LISTEN MORE AND TALK LESS.

- WHEN I FIND MYSELF CONVERSING WITH
SOMEONE I PAY ATTENTION TO MY FOCUS,
AND I TRY TO PUT ASIDE EVERYTHING ELSE
SO I CAN BE FULLY PRESENT.

- WHEN I SEE SOMEONE WHO MIGHT NEED A
HAND I ASK IF I CAN HELP.

- I AM LESS QUICK TO JUDGE OR EVALUATE
MOTIVES. IF I FIND MYSELF JUDGING I
LOOK FOR POSITIVE INTENTIONS FIRST.

- I TRY TO HAVE ONE CONVERSATION A DAY
WITH EACH OF MY TEAMMATES WHERE THE
SUBJECT IS WHAT WE ARE CREATING IN
THE WORLD AND WHO BENEFITS.

- WHEN I HAVE A PROBLEM, I MOVE TOWARD THE PROBLEM, RATHER THAN AVOIDING OR PROCRASTINATING.

- I SEEK TO BE A PERSON OF MY WORD; TO DO WHAT I SAY I WILL DO, WHEN I SAY I'LL DO IT.

- MAKE A HABIT OF THANKING OTHERS FOR WHAT THEY HAVE DONE.

- WHEN I AM WORKING WITH A CUSTOMER I MAKE AN ATTEMPT TO REMEMBER THAT THIS IS A PERSON, NOT AN OBJECT. I TRY TO AVOID CLICHÉS OR CUSTOMER SERVICE SPEAK AND CONVERSE LIKE A REGULAR HUMAN BEING.

- WHEN SOMEONE IS ACTING IN A WAY THAT IS INCONSISTENT WITH OUR MISSION, I FIND A RESPECTFUL WAY TO CALL THEM ON IT FOR THE GOOD OF THE TEAM.

John Calls a Staff Meeting

JOHN LOOKED around the table at his team. He quickly spotted the team member whose name he couldn't re-call several nights before: Cynthia. He had met Simon for coffee before the meeting. Simon suggested that he go slowly, but sitting now at the head of the table and looking at his team gave John a boost of energy.

"Good morning, everyone."

There were a few mumbled replies and Simon's clear "good morning." When notice of the meeting had circulated throughout the department, it had been met with derision by some. One summed up the general response: "So, Old Manage by Memo is actually going to sit down in the same room with us peons." But the reaction of John's team was by no means unanimous anymore. Some of the team members had been responding to John's efforts to reach out to them.

"Over the last few months our performance as a team has been unacceptable," John began.

Most heads looked down at the table.

"I have come to realize that I am a big part of the problem," he told them. "And I want to become a part of the solution. You probably noticed me out of my office more often during the weeks before the African trip. It was awkward for me and probably for you. But in order to become part of the solution, I need to get out of my office a great deal more to support you in your efforts.

"I also want to get to know you better—but only if you are willing. We depend on each other to succeed, and so many others depend on our department here at BullsEye. So I really am motivated to improve my personal performance as well as our performance as a team. Are there any questions? Yes, Marta."

"Can we get a new coffeepot? The one we have is dreadful."

The off-the-wall question caught John by surprise. "Sounds like a great idea. Anything else?"

Felix turned to Simon and said, "How was Africa? Did you get to see your family?"

That led to several minutes of animated conversation between Simon and the rest of the team about the trip. Finally John felt it necessary to say, "Okay. Let's get back to work."

As Ricardo and Scott approached their respective cubicles, Ricardo said, "That was weird. He is going to get to know us. Why? Did he get infected by something in Africa?" Little did they know how close to the truth his comment was.

John, checking the coffee machine around the corner, overheard Ricardo. He felt a surge of anger at first, which he replaced with resolve. *What else would I expect? I need to show them I've changed, not tell them.* He was accustomed to hard work, just not this kind.

During the following weeks John began each workday with a review of his strategy and his commitment to Ubuntu. He took advantage of opportunities to support his team members, engage in conversation, and develop a better understanding of their individual challenges. Over and over he raised the same questions with them:

How can we make this a better place to work?
How can I support you in what you do?
What is the purpose of our department?

How are we important to the company?
Why do we exist?

Who are our internal customers, and in what
ways do they depend on us? Who are their
customers?

How can we better serve our customers and
our customers' customers?

Will you help us develop a companywide
reputation as a team others can depend on?

What would success look like? How would it
feel to succeed?

Final Preparation for the
Corporate Presentation

Simon and John attended a series of meetings with Rolando, Steve, Kathy, and Beth Ling to prepare for their corporate presentation. At their final meeting, they intended to approve a memo inviting employees to attend the presentation and conduct one last review of their agenda.

"We probably could have done this in an e-mail," Kathy began, "but to be honest, I missed seeing all of you. Is everyone okay with the agenda?"

Everyone was.

"John, Simon, do you need any help with your portion of the presentation? Are you ready?"

"Since what I am doing is a work in progress," John said, "there is a risk that I may not have much in the way of success to point to by the time of the presentation.

If you are all willing to take that risk, I am fine with the agenda. I know that each of you has a project of your own, and I am happy to defer to you if you think that would be better."

Steve quickly replied, "I think people will respond to the authentic nature of your journey. Every leader deals with the issues you are facing in one way or another. We said we needed to educate and inspire, and I believe your story will do both.

"Let me also say I am really impressed with the way Kathy has become the embodiment of Ubuntu in our department. It has made coming to work something to look forward to."

Kathy chuckled. "I do hope the Ice Queen is melting. I agree—we should stick with John and Simon. Their story is at the heart and soul of what we hope to accomplish at BullsEye, and I think it will resonate with a lot of folks.

"Take a look at the memo we are sending to everyone."

To:	All BullsEye Employees
From:	The Africa Team (now renamed the Ubuntu Team)
Re:	All-company meeting

The team that went to Africa with the Our People Matter award winners committed to making an all-company presentation after returning. In that presentation we were asked to convey something useful that we learned in Africa that may be of value to BullsEye. We believe we did find a few useful concepts and ideas on our journey, including the African philosophy called Ubuntu.

The team believes this African philosophy can be applied to our work at BullsEye and may be beneficial as we address some of today's challenges. We believe Ubuntu speaks directly to the quality of life at BullsEye and the qualities of leadership needed to sustain high performance and personal satisfaction at work. We also believe that our customers will respond positively to BullsEye employees who embody the Ubuntu spirit, and that in turn will be good for business.

Please join us for our presentation on Friday, May 23 at 10 A.M. in the corporate auditorium in Schaumberg to find out the meaning of the greeting below:

Sawa bono.

Rolando said, "Looks great. Let's do it!" Everyone agreed.

John Gives Nancy a Progress Report

JOHN WAS nervous. It had been three weeks since his last meeting with Nancy, and though he felt he had made progress, he knew he was just getting started.

"Tell me what you have been doing, John. I understand from the other groups that the work from your team and its timeliness have improved."

John was surprised to hear that. "I am not sure why our work has improved. I haven't really accomplished all that much yet. I am simply spending more time trying to get to know my team. A few are suspicious and a couple are downright resistant, but I think I've made headway with most of them. I am staying with my plan."

"Tell me about your plan."

John took a sheet of paper out of his notebook and read the six guiding principles he'd outlined, briefly commenting on each one.

Nancy was impressed. "So what are you doing differently from before?"

"I listen to my staff, try to understand their concerns and challenges from their point of view. I also strive to keep every promise, every commitment I make. It is important to show my team that I can be trusted to do what I say I will do.

"And I am not so quick to take on things that really should be done by my employees. I'll provide support and counsel, but I trust them to do the work. For instance, Zhu Zhu told me that she was having trouble keeping track of the different client packets, so I shared an organization strategy that I had learned from BullsEye University. She is going to try it, and we will touch base tomorrow.

"I held a meeting to explore the ways we depend on one another and the ways in which our primary internal customer, BullsEye Finance, depends on us. I wasn't sure the meeting was a complete success. But it was a start."

"Do you have any additional plans?"

"I am thinking about bringing the other groups— our internal clients—in for regular conversations with my staff."

"And what do you hope to accomplish by doing that?"

"I want the team to put a human face on our work

for other departments. I want them to understand how what we do eventually reaches the ultimate customer."

"All great ideas, John. But tell me a little about your last guideline."

"Well, we spend the largest portion of our life at work. So my question is, How can we improve the quality of that part of our life? Even the most family-oriented employee spends the largest portion of his or her waking hours at work. How could I identify those things that contribute to a higher quality of life at work? So I began asking my staff what about our day-to-day life at work was positive and what was negative. A theme emerged, one that I label freedom."

"Go on."

"We have a lot of rules about what a staff person can do with his work area. I have relaxed some of those rules and allowed for a little more self-expression. And it was as if I gave them a pay raise. The boost in energy and morale was immediate. That is as far as I have gotten. But I want to continue looking for ways to give my group more freedom, to encourage morale, productivity, and self-expression. I think we all benefit from it."

"Interesting idea," Nancy said. "I must say, it seems to be working. What I see is that you are trying quite a few ways to connect with and support your staff."

"I guess I have. I certainly spend more time getting to know them. I learned that Scott's son made the varsity basketball team and had the most rebounds in the first game. Talk about a proud dad.

"And some of the conversations have resulted in

some great work ideas, coincidentally. I discovered that one of our most vexing process glitches could be eliminated with better up-front communication with our customers. We are working with the other groups to put this into practice. Barb is already on board."

"Great!"

"To think that not long ago I thought I had to have all the answers."

"And I guess by now you have identified the weak members of the team."

"Yes," John responded.

"I am guessing Ricardo is one."

"Ricardo is a challenge but not the weakest member of the team."

"Then who is?

"Me."

John and Nancy both laughed appreciatively.

"Well, if that's true, John, you seem to be making progress with the weak member of your team, as you call him. I am officially taking your reassignment off the table. Let's consider you a probationary occupant of your position pending further progress reviews. Let me know how I can support you. I believe you are on the right track, John. And you can't imagine my relief."

As John stood and headed for the door, Nancy asked, "How is Simon, by the way?"

He paused and responded, "He continues to be incredibly helpful. We have been working on the corporate presentation."

"August 23. I will be there."

John Begins His Most
Ambitious Project

JOHN DECIDED it was time to deal directly with Ricardo. Since he hadn't had much success so far, he decided to jump in and let Ubuntu values guide his conversation.

Originally he had thought he had two serious employee challenges. But Marta, his other concern, had begun to respond to his efforts and even seemed enthusiastic about making the department one on which everyone at BullsEye could depend. He sensed that Simon had played a role in this after seeing Simon offering Marta assistance one afternoon. He later discovered that Simon had covered for Marta when her daughter was sick and she needed to leave early. But Ricardo stayed distant and unresponsive.

"Ricardo, will you join me in the conference room? Can I get you a cup of coffee on the way?"

"I don't drink coffee."

John let it go at that and headed for the conference room, where he took a seat at the round table near the door. Ricardo took a seat at the long table. John thought, Oh, boy.

Ricardo had left the door open. John closed it, saying, "I would like this to be just between the two of us." When he came back, he sat across from Ricardo.

"I know what you are doing," Ricardo opened. "You are singling me out as the bad guy."

"What do you mean, Ricardo?"

"I see you making nice to everyone else. And they are falling for it."

"Well, you're right. I have been avoiding you, Ricardo."

"That's what I'm saying."

"I have avoided you because I didn't know where to begin. I am not proud of that. You seem to have so little respect for me that I didn't know what to do. Today I decided just to jump in. That is why I asked you to join me. I want to find out how I have failed you."

"Say what?"

"I must have let you down somewhere along the way."

"That's right."

"So tell me how, Ricardo."

"Why you want to know?"

"I am trying hard to improve. The rumors about my possibly being fired or demoted were true. But that has passed, and it looks like I am going to be around for a while. That means we will continue to be working together. I want to know what I have done wrong so I can improve. Does that make sense?"

"Okay. I'll tell you the first thing you did. I asked you for something important, and you didn't even listen to me. I asked for a favor, and you blew me off."

"When?"

"It was our first month together. I asked you if I could have time off to attend a funeral. You asked if it was family, and I told you 'sort of family.' You said it is either family or not family, that it couldn't be both, and time off for funerals was allowed only for immediate family."

"Whose funeral was it, Ricardo?"

"A guy I knew at the last foster home I was in. I can't count the number of foster homes I lived in after I was taken away from my parents. When I arrived at the Ludders, I was twelve. I was lost. They turned out to be good people, though, and I stayed with them through high school. Their son Adam and I were like brothers. We were the same age. He wasn't blood family, but to me he was family."

"How did he die?"

"Motorcycle accident. A car ran a red light at an intersection."

"I'm sorry, Ricardo."

"Too late, man."

"I know I can't undo what I did. I was a new manager and trying to follow company policy. But that is no excuse. I should have listened to you more carefully. I should have asked more questions. I could have been a better manager and a more compassionate human being. But I wasn't. All I can do now is try to do a better job in the future. Will you give me a chance?"

"Don't know. Maybe. Can I go now?"

"Yes. Thank you for being straight with me. I appreciate your honesty."

John sat in the empty conference room, thinking about the conversation. He thought, Now I know how this began. I can't undo it. I owe Ricardo some patience, but how much? How long do I wait before I have to deal with Ricardo's performance issue? Geez, I was a piece of work as a manager. Thank goodness for Simon.

The Corporate Presentation

THERE WAS a buzz in the auditorium. Most of the seats were occupied. The ten weeks had passed in a flash, and it was show time.

After a few high-pitched squeals from the microphone, Sylvana addressed the audience. "Part of our agreement with the OPM winners was that they would bring back something from Africa. It was to be something they felt could help at BullsEye under the broad initiative of Our People Matter. I know they took this charge seriously, because they began planning their presentation immediately upon their return. I am excited to see what they brought home with them. Let's hear from our Africa adventurers!"

Kathy accepted the handheld microphone. "Thank you, Sylvana, and thank all of you for coming here this morning. To all of you who are watching on closed circuit television or who will view this program on DVD, thank you for your time and attention.

Well, our journey to South Africa did turn out to be the trip of a lifetime—and all the more so because we believe we have brought back some ideas, born in Africa, that have the capacity to make a significant contribution to BullsEye, to our customers, and to those of us who work here.

"First we would like to tell you about our journey. Let's start with some visuals to give you a context for our presentation."

With that, the lights dimmed and Kathy took them

on a brief tour of the places and people the group had visited and met. There were oohs and aaahs after the footage of the baby elephant but only silence as she showed the dramatic pictures of Soweto and that city's pride and poverty.

As the lights were turned back up, Kathy began talking, emotion cracking her voice. "I am of African descent, but I knew so little about South Africa. In Soweto the enormity of what happened in South Africa became clear to all of us. I knew the words—apartheid, reconciliation, Mandela, Bishop Tutu—but I didn't know the details. Apartheid was one of the most horrible political atrocities ever imposed on a people.

"As apartheid came to an end, something unexpected and beautiful came to pass. The decades of apartheid did not end in a bloody revolution, as history might predict. There was an ingredient in the African mindset that was large enough, wise enough, and compassionate enough to prevent such a harsh response. It is called Ubuntu.

"Nelson Mandela, Desmond Tutu, and others drew from the deep African wisdom of Ubuntu in their time of greatest need. And we are convinced that Ubuntu can make a positive difference here at BullsEye.

"One of my fellow travelers, Simon, was born and raised in Africa. His knowledge helped us understand the principles more clearly, from a native son's perspective. We owe Simon special recognition. I won't ask you to applaud, because Simon is rather shy."

116

The applause nonetheless was loud and extended. Although Simon kept his eyes down, there was a look of pleasure on his face.

"I am going to ask you to join us in a simple exercise. We want you to ask yourself the same question we asked ourselves in a discussion that preceded what you might call a moment of truth in Africa. You can jot down your answers or just keep them in your head. The question is: What things do you most want present in the life you spend at work?"

Kathy repeated the question and then paused as people in the audience shouted out their responses. When she once again had everyone's attention, she asked, "By a show of hands, who listed 'respect' as one of your answers?"

About two-thirds of the audience raised their hands.

"How about 'trust'?"

Again, a great many hands in the auditorium went up.

"Honesty?"

At least half the hands were in the air.

"Satisfaction or fulfillment?

Most hands are were raised.

"Money?"

Amid sustained laughter, most hands were raised.

"You might make money without Ubuntu, but financial success is also on the list.

"All of these qualities are directly related to Ubuntu. Ubuntu is a philosophy that embraces what we most want in our lives, including our life at work. In a sense,

Ubuntu contains the formula for a human happiness. It has the potential to create a way of being at work that will allow us to scale to new heights in how we treat each other *and* how we perform as a company. That's what we brought back to share with you today: Ubuntu. We brought home an idea that can make our lives better and at the same time boost results. Steve, Rolando. Want to pick it up from here?"

The two of them walked to the podium, looking very distinguished in their African robes.

"Thanks, Kathy," Steve said. "So what is Ubuntu? Simply stated, it's a philosophy of unity and purpose where our actions demonstrate a recognition and understanding that we are all connected. When we embrace Ubuntu, we choose to treat each other in an open, honest, and respectful way while working to achieve our goals. We respect each person's humanity regardless of our differences. It's the spirit of humanity that allows us to empathize with each other and enables us to make a difference together in our lives and in our goals here at work."

"And Ubuntu is available to each of us," Rolando added. "The values it is based on can influence our thoughts, behaviors, and actions. We have seen firsthand how it can break down barriers between people and foster the pursuit of common goals."

"So what does embracing Ubuntu mean on a practical basis?" Steve continued. "Our workplace language is full of words like 'management,' 'supervision,' 'innovation,' 'strategy,' 'coordination,' 'facilitation,' 'motivation,' 'recognition,' and even 'big hairy audacious goals.'

And they all refer to important aspects of running a successful company.

"Ubuntu represents a foundation or platform of values that allows most of those processes to function more effectively while at the same time improving the quality of life at work. Not a bad deal. Ubuntu has already demonstrated it can change the world. It can enhance our lives and improve our results at BullsEye.

"We all know that being 'rewarded,' 'motivated,' or 'managed' by someone who has not connected with us at a human level often feels like manipulation. Ubuntu is about finding the common ground that connects one human to another. It is about accepting each human being as a unique and valuable member of the human community and respecting the humanity of each and every person we encounter. It fosters teamwork and cooperation and the contribution of every member of a team.

"Ubuntu isn't a standard corporate program. Ubuntu is about how you can engage others in the human-to-human part of your work life. It is an attitude and a way of thinking.

"So how do we help create Ubuntu? How do we implement it if it is voluntary? I want you to meet two of our own BullsEye employees who have an Ubuntu story to tell. John, Simon."

John and Simon Tell Their Story

THIS REMARKABLE man next to me has been my guide on the most important journey of my life," John began. "I didn't just go to Africa; Africa came to me first. Ubuntu helped me save my job."

The room became quiet.

John proceeded to tell quickly the story of his difficulties in managing his department and getting results from his people. He described how he compensated with long hours until that, too, wasn't enough. In an emotion-drained voice, he described the impact of his struggles at work on his family and his ultimate separation from his wife and daughter. He described the weekend when Simon emerged as his teacher. He even disclosed a bit about his childhood, growing up in a small Minnesota town and working in a small family business.

"I first heard the word 'Ubuntu' when Simon used it to describe his reason for coming to my assistance over the holiday weekend even though his personal work was flawless. Our discussions led me to see things from a different perspective. My beliefs about people were helping to bring about the very actions that were threatening my job and destroying my family life. I had this hard-nosed belief that because you get a paycheck, you therefore work tirelessly at your job. I didn't see my team as people but as workers, cogs in the wheel. I didn't understand the connection between leadership and a world in which we are all connected. My outlook and the way I work have changed thanks to Simon and Ubuntu.

"What happened next was even more amazing."

Simon now reached for the microphone. "I grew up with Ubuntu as a member of the Zulu clan in Africa. As a child I lived through apartheid and rejoiced at the reconciliation. And just when I thought life couldn't get any better, I was given an opportunity to come to the U.S. and continue my schooling. I have learned a great deal in my MBA program. I believe that the things I have been studying will someday be of great value. The surprise to me was that something I took for granted in my life turned out to have value to my boss, my colleagues, and my company. Ubuntu has always been of value to me, but I hadn't paid special attention to it because it was always there, like the water a fish swims in.

"I was lucky enough to win the OPM top prize and return to Africa with this group you have just heard from. And I watched them discover the wisdom embedded in the African culture I grew up in. And I rediscovered it myself through their eyes. I have never felt such pride for my country or for my company. I want to tell you how proud I am to work for and be a part of this organization. When I eventually return to my homeland, I will be taking many important things with me, gifts from each of you. I hope you will discover Ubuntu for yourself and see that it will help you as it has helped me.

"John has identified a number of specific principles in Ubuntu which he has been using as a guide as he forges anew his relationships at work. He was on probation and about to be removed from management. Last week, because of his progress over the last ten weeks, he was removed from probation. Our department has improved its performance in every category. And in the last week his new outlook on life has led to the thawing of his relationship with his wife. He believes he has Ubuntu to thank. That is our story."

The entire audience rose as one and responded to Simon's speech with thunderous applause. Steve, Rolando, and Kathy joined John and Simon on stage as the applause died, giving each other hugs, handshakes, and high fives. Then Kathy took the microphone.

"We want to start a companywide conversation about Ubuntu and its possibilities for BullsEye. We learned from the employee survey a few months ago that many in our workforce are dissatisfied. We believe that dissatisfaction has affected both the bottom line of our company and the way we serve our customers.

"In our discussions following our trip to South Africa, we decided unanimously that Ubuntu must start at a personal level. So let's begin the conversation about Ubuntu here. Let me ask you, Have you ever experienced anything like Ubuntu? What was its impact on you?"

Microphones had been set up throughout the room so that everyone's comments could be heard clearly. People shared, for the most part, simple stories of thanks they had received from those they worked with and how it made them feel. A theme emerged. When recognition was given in a respectful way, it had a big impact on an individual's morale and sense of purpose. One woman described a handwritten note she had been given by a supervisor ten years ago; she keeps it posted over her desk to this day.

Others talked about the family atmosphere that existed in their work environment and how colleagues in their work community never hesitated to help one another, often without being asked.

The CEO Adds His Story

IN THE back of the room a tall man rose from his seat— BullsEye's CEO, Len Dufore. "Yes, Mr. Dufore," Kathy said. A stillness replaced the buzz, and all heads turned.

"First, I want to thank the team that went to South Africa. Flyaway Airlines, as well, has been a terrific partner. I look forward to hearing about and participating in anything that could make our BullsEye community a more human, caring, and cooperative and successful place to work. I am confident that we would reap the benefits from Ubuntu both personally and corporate-wide and that our customers would be better served, as well.

"So much for the CEO-speak. I really mean what I just said, but it probably is the sort of thing you expect to hear from me. Now I want to talk from the heart.

"John and I share a similar experience. I had been with BullsEye for fifteen years when something happened that dramatically affected my worldview.

"I was being considered for a promotion I expected to receive. Oh, the brashness of youth. I didn't receive the promotion; Bob Morris did. You may recognize that name as he is our current chairman of the board. Bob was given the job I thought should be mine, and he became an excellent senior VP of sales and later a fine CEO. But at the time it felt like a setback for me. I began to have some personal doubts, which I salted with a generous dash of self-pity. It was the first real setback of my career, and I didn't handle it well. If you worked with me at that time, I am sorry, because I don't think it was a pleasant experience. I was later told there were discussions about letting me go.

"Late one evening I was working on a critical project that would lead to a significant expansion of BullsEye outside of the U.S., I couldn't seem to focus. My mind kept revisiting my failed promotion. So I decided to take a walk.

"In the corridor I ran into a woman who was cleaning. We struck up a conversation, and I asked her about her job and about her family. She said she was working two jobs. I asked about her husband and learned she was a single mom with three children. She hoped she was doing what was best for her family by working two jobs and asking her mother for help with the children. She told me proudly that her children were in a private school and getting good grades. We must have talked for half an hour.

"During the conversation I asked her why she didn't ask me what I did. She said she knew what I did and was amazed that I was talking with her. I asked why. And she said that it was because I was a 'higher-up' and the higher-ups rarely notice the 'little people.' The way she said 'little people' has bothered me to this day.

"When I returned to my office, I had my energy back and my self-pity was gone. I thought about the woman's comments and how I must look as a 'higher-up.' From that day forward I made it a point to let each person I meet know by my actions that on a human level I do not see little people and higher-ups but only fellow human beings with different responsibilities. I believe we are all connected in the most essential ways. Some may be paid more or less depending on the market value of the skills and experiences we bring to BullsEye, our education, and the varying degrees of responsibility we assume. But we all deserve the same level of respect from one another. There are no little people.

"And now you have brought us a philosophy that contains and expands upon this idea: Ubuntu. I hope from this day forward we can each find a way to make Ubuntu a part of our company and our culture as we go about our daily tasks.

ubuntu!

As long as there are employees who think of themselves as "little people," the work of Ubuntu is not finished.

"Last year we received the worst survey ratings from you we have had since we started collecting employee feedback. Recession or no recession, that is unacceptable. I accept responsibility for not seeing what was happening. But I need your help in solving the problem. BullsEye can and should be a great place to work.

I believe in these ideas. But this has to be something we do together.

"Thank you."

The applause was loud and sustained. It was widely known that the CEO sat behind a standard-issue desk much like their own, in a standard-sized office. Now BullsEye's employees knew why he made that choice.

In the Aftermath of the Presentation

To:	The Ubuntu Team
From:	Kathy
Subject:	Postpresentation Meeting
Attendees:	John, Simon, Beth, Rolando, Kathy, Steve, and Len

It was great to have Len at our follow-up meeting. He supports our efforts and our nonprogram approach. Below is a summary of our conclusions regarding spreading the message of Ubuntu throughout BullsEye.

1.   The best way for someone to learn about the message and impact of Ubuntu is to experience it firsthand. We must provide opportunities and encouragement for that to happen: setting up opportunities to get to know one another, sharing information that is important to our mutual success, asking for each employee's input and feedback.

2.   The best way to spread the message of Ubuntu is to create a nucleus of people who embrace Ubuntu in all

aspects of our lives, starting at work. As the circle grows, so will Ubuntu's impact.

3.   Ubuntu cannot come across as just another management initiative. We must be clear that Ubuntu is a philosophy, one with enormous potential to improve life at BullsEye.

4.   There needs to be an element of fun in what we do to energize others and help us bond.

5.   We should invite and inspire others to join us as we re-create BullsEye in light of Ubuntu. How? By modeling behaviors that reflect the spirit of recognition and cooperation and teamwork and equity that is Ubuntu.

6.   We must never forget that this is an ongoing long-term effort, not one with a specific time frame. We must build Ubuntu within BullsEye one conversation at a time.

Thanks for your participation. I think we are off to a great start.

Ubuntu Growth Opportunities

INITIALLY, THE impact of Ubuntu within BullsEye became evident in the increased cooperation and teamwork exhibited by colleagues and employees in the daily operations and interactions of the company. Before long, however, the principles and values underlying Ubuntu began to become evident beyond the workplace, as well. The community-based activities that HR and the Ubuntu Group made available were quick to be embraced, from visiting BullsEye retirees, to volunteer training for hospice programs, to the adopt a school program, to the BullsEye day at the Our Table soup kitchen.

Other kinds of programs the Ubuntu Group worked to create included the popular "Immersion Experiences," a day walking in another's shoes in which BullsEye employees were given a chance to shadow police officers, social workers, and others who provide critical services to the community; a Special Olympics program for physically handicapped kids; and the Timber Zulu Soweto Project, in which BullsEye employees helped collect and send books, school supplies, used computers, toys, and other materials to the children of Soweto and other impoverished communities throughout the world.

Six Months Later

YOU CAN feel the difference," Steve noted.

Steve, Rolando, and Kathy were catching up over coffee at their usual hangout.

"What do you see, Steve?"

"I'm not sure how to describe it, but BullsEye has more energy. People are more alive. There is a sense of calm and cooperation and civility—of community—at headquarters. The atmosphere is more like that of a healthy family than a company. You hear laughter on the floors. People greet each other whether they know you or not."

"I've experienced the same thing, Steve," Kathy said. "How about you, Rolando?"

"Yes. It is amazing to me when I remember what BullsEye was like before."

"Do you think it will last?"

"We can only hope Ubuntu takes root, Steve. The volunteer groups have become incredibly popular. There is a waiting list now to join. Hopefully, these kinds of experiences will begin to anchor Ubuntu in our daily lives. The worst that can happen is that we do a lot of good in the community and make BullsEye a friendlier place to work. But ideally, we'll continue to become a better, stronger, more successful company, and the spirit of helpfulness and teamwork and cooperation we've fostered will continue to deliver strong results to the bottom line and increased customer loyalty."

A Year Later in Barrington

THANKS FOR bringing that to my attention, Ricardo. Do you have a minute to update me on your project with Nicole?"

"Sure. What would you like to know?"

"How long do you think it will take to finish?"

"We should be finished next week."

"Ahead of schedule again."

"Yes. Well, we have been getting some terrific help

129

from the other team members in our department. I love the way everyone works together to help one another. To me, that is the most visible impact of Ubuntu on the company. A year ago, who would believe other people would help me with my work?"

"I have noticed that you've been finding ways to be of help to others, too."

Ricardo just shrugged.

"Well, thanks for the update. Are you going dancing tonight?"

"It's Friday, John. Where else would I be?"

A few minutes later John encountered Nicole. "Good night, Nicole. Have a good weekend. By the way, Ricardo says you guys are almost done. Nice work."

"That Ricardo is a stitch. He can be so funny! Who knew? The tough guy is a pussycat. What are you doing this weekend?"

"My daughter and I are going to visit my parents at the assisted living center. How about you?"

"Nothing much. Helping around the house. We may take in a movie. With the snow forecast, I want to stay close to home. Say, John, I so enjoyed meeting your family when they visited during the holidays. Next time bring your new dog, Bo."

"If the cleaning crew will let me: golden retrievers really shed."

As John approached the elevator bank, he saw that the box created for books to be sent to Soweto was almost full. He smiled and punched the elevator button.

Simon Says Farewell

S IMON GRADUATED with his MBA in the spring, and he and Sarah began making plans for their return to Africa. He wanted to say good-bye personally to everyone he had worked with and met in helping to spread the message and values of Ubuntu throughout BullsEye but realized there were simply too many people. So he drafted an open letter that was posted on the company's internal website. His letter found its way to every corner of the BullsEye Corporation.

To My BullsEye Family,

It is with heavy heart that I say good-bye to you. Yet that sadness is tempered by the great joy my wife Sarah and I feel about going home. I came to America to learn more about management and business and to experience the working life of Americans. I feel I've learned a great deal. But perhaps my greatest education has been working with all of you at BullsEye, to make BullsEye a better and more successful company. I leave you with a deep sense of gratitude—it has been an experience I will always cherish.

I didn't expect to leave anything behind that others might find of value. But I discovered that something as familiar to me as the air I breathe—Ubuntu—could be of value to those who gave me so much. I leave the spirit of Ubuntu in your hands. In doing so, I would like to leave you with a few thoughts about Ubuntu that may be helpful.

—Simon

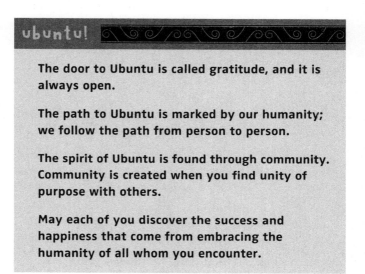

ubuntu!

The door to Ubuntu is called gratitude, and it is always open.

The path to Ubuntu is marked by our humanity; we follow the path from person to person.

The spirit of Ubuntu is found through community. Community is created when you find unity of purpose with others.

May each of you discover the success and happiness that come from embracing the humanity of all whom you encounter.

ACKNOWLEDGMENTS

S TEPHEN would like to once again acknowledge the steadfast support of my wife and best friend, Janell, whose journals were a source of much descriptive material about Soweto. The authors would also like to recognize the amazing Broadway team headed by Roger Scholl.

—STEPHEN C. LUNDIN, Ph.D.
BOB NELSON, Ph.D.

About the Authors

DR. STEPHEN LUNDIN is a writer, public speaker, entrepreneur, and filmmaker with a rich history as a graduate-level business school professor and dean. Steve has written a number of books including the multimillion-copy bestselling *Fish!* and the simply bestselling *Fish! Tales, Fish! Sticks,* and *Fish! for Life. Top Performer: A Bold Approach to Sales and Service; CATS: The Nine Lives of Innovation;* and *Loops: The Seven Keys to Small Business Success* are more recent publications.

During the last decade Steve has worked with hundreds of companies in over forty-five countries. The government of Abu Dhabi, nursing homes in New Zealand, banking systems in Africa, Australia, and Malaysia, a shipping company in Singapore, the Japanese, Singapore, and Australian Management Institutes, and health-club chains in Sweden and Portugal are a few of his clients along with top U.S. companies and nonprofits. He can be reached at slrunner@aol.com. His blog can be found at www.loops4biz.com.

BOB NELSON provides consulting, keynote presentations, and management training through his company, Nelson Motivation Inc. For more information, to register for his free Tip of the Week, or to order any of his books or related products at bulk discounts, contact:

> Nelson Motivation Inc.
> P.O. Box 500872
> San Diego, CA 92150-9973
> 1-800-575-5521 (toll free)
> www.nelson-motivation.com

You can reach Bob directly at 858-673-0690 in San Diego or via the Internet at bobrewards@aol.com.